BASIC

ENGLISH
GRAMMAR

Second Edition

Volume A

Betty Schrampfer Azar

Longman

Library of Congress Cataloging-in-Publication Data

Azar, Betty Schrampfer, 1941-
   Basic English grammar / Betty Schrampfer Azar. -- 2nd ed.
     p.   cm.
   Includes indexes.
   ISBN 0-13-368424-5 (v. 1). -- ISBN 0-13-368358-3 (v. 2)
   1. English language--Textbooks for foreign speakers. 2. English
language--Grammar--Problems, exercises, etc.   I. Title
PE1128.A96   1995
428.2'4--dc20   92-25711
                                  CIP

Publisher: *Tina B. Carver*
Editorial/Production Supervision: *Janet Johnston*
Editorial Assistant: *Shelley Hartle*
Manufacturing Manager: *Ray Keating*
Art Director: *Merle Krumper*
Cover Design: *Joel Mitnick Design*
Interior Design: *Ros Herion Freese*
Illustrations: *Don Martinetti*

A Pearson Education Company
Pearson Education
10 Bank Street
White Plains, NY 10606

Printed in the United States of America.

10 9 8

ISBN 0-13-368424-5

Contents

Chapter 3   EXPRESSING PRESENT TIME (PART 2)

Chapter 4   NOUNS AND PRONOUNS

Chapter 5 EXPRESSING PAST TIME

Preface to the Second Edition

Basic English Grammar remains a developmental skills text for students of English as a second or foreign language. Serving as both a reference and a workbook, it introduces students to the form, meaning, and usage of basic structures in English. It provides ample opportunities for practice through extensive and varied exercises leading to communicative activities. Although it focuses on grammar, it promotes the development of all language skills.

This second edition has a greatly expanded range of contents to provide a solid core of basic English grammar for lower-level or beginning students. It includes numerous new exercises with, at the end of each chapter, cumulative review exercises that include additional communicative and interactive student-centered tasks.

Also available are an *Answer Key*, with answers only, and a *Teacher's Guide*, with teaching suggestions as well as the answers to the exercises.

Acknowledgments

Writing English grammar texts is a pleasure for me. In this pursuit, I am helped by many wonderful people: dedicated teachers who give presentations at conferences and write articles for regional newsletters or international journals; researchers who explore the hows and whys of second language acquisition; grammarians who present their observations clearly and convincingly; past and present authors of other ESL/EFL grammar materials who show creative and sound approaches to helping students gain understanding and usage ability of English; colleagues who give me valuable feedback and share their pedagogical insights; and publishing professionals who know how to mold and market educational materials. We all rely on one another.

Above all, I am indebted to my students, who have taught me a great deal about the language acquisition process by openly sharing with me their learning experiences and practical needs.

In sum, I am indebted to the ESL/EFL community of teachers, researchers, authors, publishers, and students.

In particular, I thank Tina Carver, Janet Johnston, and Shelley Hartle for their invaluable professionalism as well as friendship. I also wish to thank Barbara Matthies, Irene Juzkiw, Stacy Hagen, Nancy Price, Lawrence Cisar, Don Martinetti, Lizette Reyes, Stella Reilly, Marita Froimson, Joy Edwards, R.T. Steltz, Sue Van Etten, Ken Kortlever, Generessa Arielle, and Chelsea Azar. My gratitude goes also to the many wonderful teachers and publishers I met in Korea, Japan, and Taiwan on my trip to Asia in 1994.

CHAPTER 1
Using *Be* and *Have*

■ **EXERCISE 1:** Learn the names of your classmates and teacher. Write their names in the spaces below.

_____   _____

_____   _____

_____   _____

_____   _____

_____   _____

_____   _____

_____   _____

_____   _____

_____   _____

_____   _____

_____   _____

1-1 NOUN + *IS* + NOUN: SINGULAR

NOUN + *IS* + NOUN
(a) ***Canada   is*** a ***country.***
	"Singular" means "one, not two or more."
	In (a): *Canada* = a singular noun
	  is = a singular verb
	  country = a singular noun

(b) Mexico is ***a c***ountry.	***A*** frequently comes in front of singular nouns. In (b): ***a*** comes in front of the singular noun *country*. ***A*** is called "an article."
(c) ***A*** cat is ***an a***nimal.	***A*** and ***an*** have the same meaning. They are both articles. ***A*** is used in front of words that begin with consonants: *b, c, d, f, g, h, j, k, etc.* Examples: *a bed, a cat, a dog, a friend, a girl* ***An*** is used in front of words that begin with *a, e, i,* and *o.*★ Examples: *an animal, an ear, an island, an office*

★***An*** is also sometimes used in front of words that begin with *u.* See Chart 4-7.
The letters *a, e, i, o,* and *u* are called "vowels."
All of the other letters in the alphabet are called "consonants."

■ **EXERCISE 2:** Complete the sentences. Use an ARTICLE, ***a*** or ***an***.

1. ___*A*___ horse is ___*an*___ animal.

2. English is _____ language.

3. Chicago is _____ city.

4. Korea is _____ country.

5. Europe is _____ continent.

6. _____ dictionary is _____ book.

7. _____ hotel is _____ building.

8. _____ bear is _____ animal.

9. _____ bee is _____ insect.

10. _____ ant is _____ insect.

■ **EXERCISE 3:** Complete the sentences. Use an ARTICLE (***a*** or ***an***) and the words in the list.

animal	*continent*	*insect*
city	*country*	*language*

1. Arabic is _____*a language*_____ .

2. Rome is _____*a city*_____ .

3. A cat is _____*an animal*_____ .

4. Asia is _____ .

5. Tokyo is _____ .

6. Spanish is _____ .

7. Mexico is _____ .

8. London is _____ .

9. A bee is _____ .

10. South America is _____ .

11. A dog is _____ .

12. China is _____ .

13. Russian is _____ .

14. A cow is _____ .

15. A fly is _____ .

■ **EXERCISE 4—ORAL:** Complete the sentences with your own words. Think of more than one possible completion.

1. . . . is a language.
   → *English is a language.*
   → *Spanish is a language.*
   → *Arabic is a language.*
   → *Etc.*

2. . . . is a country.

3. . . . is a city.

4. . . . is a continent.

5. . . . is an animal.

6. . . . is an insect.

1-2 NOUN + *ARE* + NOUN: PLURAL

NOUN + *ARE* + NOUN (a) **Cats** **are** **animals.**	"Plural" means "two, three, or more." *Cats* = a plural noun *are* = a plural verb *animals* = a plural noun
(b) SINGULAR: a cat, an animal. PLURAL: cat**s**, animal**s**	Plural nouns end in *-s*. *A* and *an* are used only with singular nouns.
(c) SINGULAR: a ci**ty**, a coun**try**. PLURAL: ci**ties**, coun**tries**	Some singular nouns that end in *-y* have a special plural form: They omit the *-y* and add *-ies*.★
NOUN *and* NOUN + *ARE* + NOUN (d) **Canada and** **China** **are** **countries.** (e) **Dogs** **and** **cats** **are** **animals.**	Two nouns connected by *and* are followed by *are*. In (d): *Canada* is a singular noun. *China* is a singular noun. They are connected by *and*. Together they are plural, i.e., "more than one."

★See Chart 2-6 for more information about adding *-s/-es* to words that end in *-y*.

■ **EXERCISE 5:** Change the singular sentences to plural sentences.

SINGULAR   PLURAL

1. An ant is an insect.   →   <u> Ants are insects. </u>

2. A computer is a machine.   →   _____

3. A dictionary is a book.   →   _____

4. A chicken is a bird.   →   _____

5. A rose is a flower.   →   _____

6. A carrot is a vegetable.   →   _____

7. A rabbit is an animal.   →   _____

■ **EXERCISE 6:** Complete the sentences with *is* or *are* and one of the nouns in the list. Use the correct singular form of the noun (using *a* or *an*) or the correct plural form.

animal	country	language
city	insect	machine
continent		

1. A dog _____ *is an animal* _____.

2. Dogs _____ *are animals* _____.

3. Spanish _____.

4. Spanish and Chinese _____.

5. Asia _____.

6. Asia and Africa _____.

7. Thailand and Viet Nam _____.

8. Thailand _____.

9. Butterflies _____.

10. A butterfly _____.

11. An automobile _____.

12. Automobiles _____.

13. London _____.

14. London and Baghdad _____.

■ **EXERCISE 7—ORAL:** Complete the sentences with your own words.

Example: . . . a country.
Response: (Brazil is) a country.

1. . . . a country.
2. . . . countries.
3. . . . languages.
4. . . . a language.
5. . . . a city.
6. . . . cities.
7. . . . animals.
8. . . . an insect.
9. . . . a peninsula.
10. . . . streets in this city.
11. . . . countries in Asia.
12. . . . a city in Europe.
13. . . . a plant.
14. . . . a vegetable.
15. . . . a season.

■ **EXERCISE 8—ORAL (BOOKS CLOSED):** What are the following things?

Example: Cows
Response: Cows are animals.

1. English
2. England
3. Butterflies
4. Chickens
5. Europe
6. Roses
7. A carrot
8. Russian and Arabic
9. Spring
10. Japan and Venezuela
11. A computer
12. A bear
13. Bees
14. An ant
15. Winter and summer
16. September and October
17. A dictionary
18. Typewriters
19. A Honda
20. *(names of cars, cities, countries, continents, animals, insects)*

1-3 PRONOUN + *BE* + NOUN

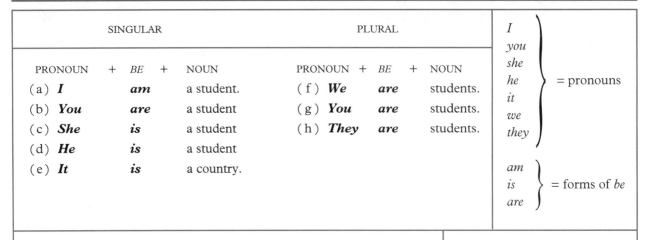

	SINGULAR				PLURAL			
	PRONOUN	+ *BE* +	NOUN		PRONOUN	+ *BE* +	NOUN	*I* *you* *she* *he* } = pronouns *it* *we* *they*
(a)	*I*	am	a student.	(f)	*We*	are	students.	
(b)	*You*	are	a student	(g)	*You*	are	students.	*am* *is* } = forms of *be* *are*
(c)	*She*	is	a student	(h)	*They*	are	students.	
(d)	*He*	is	a student					
(e)	*It*	is	a country.					

(i) *Rita* is in my class. **She** is a student.	Pronouns refer to nouns.
(j) *Tom* is in my class. **He** is a student.	In (i): *she* (feminine) = Rita
(k) *Rita and Tom* are in my class. **They** are students.	In (j): *he* (masculine) = Tom
	In (k): *they* = Rita and Tom

■ **EXERCISE 9:** Complete the sentences. Use a VERB: *am*, *is*, or *are*. Use a NOUN: *a student* or *students*.

1. We _____*are students*_____.

2. I _____.

3. Rita goes to school. She _____.

4. Rita and Tom go to school. They _____.

5. You *(one person)* _____.

6. You *(two persons)* _____.

■ **EXERCISE 10—ORAL (BOOKS CLOSED):** Complete the sentences with *a form of* **be** + *a* ***student/students.*** Indicate the subject or subjects with your hand.

> *Example:* (. . .) *(The teacher supplies the name of a student.)*
> *Response:* (Yoko) is a student. *(The responding student indicates Yoko.)*

1. (. . .)   6. (. . .)
2. (. . .) and (. . .)   7. (. . .) and (. . .)
3. I   8. They
4. (. . .) and I   9. You
5. We   10. (. . .) and (. . .) and (. . .)

Now identify the given people as students and, in addition, tell what country or continent they are from.

11. (. . .)
     → *(Yoko) is a student. She is from Japan.*
12. (. . .) and (. . .)
     → *(Luis) and (Pablo) are students. They are from South America.*
13. (. . .)
14. (. . .) and (. . .)
15. Etc.

1-4 CONTRACTIONS WITH *BE*

	PRONOUN	+	*BE*	→	CONTRACTION			When people speak, they often push two words together. *A contraction* = two words that are pushed together.
AM	I	+	am	→	***I'm***	(a)	***I'm*** a student.	
IS	she	+	is	→	***she's***	(b)	***She's*** a student.	Contractions of a *subject pronoun* + **be** are used in both speaking and writing.
	he	+	is	→	***he's***	(c)	***He's*** a student.	
	it	+	is	→	***it's***	(d)	***It's*** a city.	
ARE	you	+	are	→	***you're***	(e)	***You're*** a student. ***You're*** students.	PUNCTUATION: The mark in the middle of a contraction is called an "apostrophe" (').
	we	+	are	→	***we're***	(f)	***We're*** students.	
	they	+	are	→	***they're***	(g)	***They're*** students.	

NOTE: Write an apostrophe above the line. Do not write an apostrophe on the line.

CORRECT: _____ *I'm a student.* _____

INCORRECT: _____ *I,m a student.* _____

■ **EXERCISE 11:** Complete the sentences. Use CONTRACTIONS (*pronoun* + *be*).

1. *Sara* is a student. _____She's_____ in my class.

2. *Jim* is a student. _____ in my class.

3. I have *one brother.* _____ twenty years old.

4. I have *two sisters.* _____ students.

5. I have *a dictionary.* _____ on my desk.

6. I like *my classmates.* _____ friendly.

7. I have *three books.* _____ on my desk.

8. *My brother* is twenty-six years old. _____ married.

9. *My sister* is twenty-one years old. _____ single.

10. *Yoko and Ali* are students. _____ in my class.

11. I like *my books.* _____ interesting.

12. I like *grammar.* _____ easy.

13. *Kate and I* live in an apartment. _____ roommates.

14. We live in *an apartment.* _____ on Pine Street.

15. *I* go to school. _____ a student.

16. I know *you.* _____ in my English class.

1-5 NEGATIVE WITH *BE*

(a) Tom $\begin{bmatrix} \textit{is not} \\ \textit{isn't} \end{bmatrix}$ a teacher. He is a student.	*Not* makes a sentence negative. *Not* can be contracted with *is* and *are*: CONTRACTION: *is* + *not* = *isn't* CONTRACTION: *are* + *not* = *aren't*
(b) Tom and Ann $\begin{bmatrix} \textit{are not} \\ \textit{aren't} \end{bmatrix}$ teachers.	
(c) I *am not* a teacher.	*Am* and *not* are not contracted.

■ **EXERCISE 12:** Complete the sentences with the correct information.

1. Korea _____*isn't*_____ a city. It *'s a country*_____.

2. Horses _____ insects. They _____.

3. Asia _____ a country. It _____.

4. Bees and ants _____ animals. They _____.

5. Arabic _____ a country. It _____.

6. I _____ a professional photographer. I _____.

Ms. Black

Jim

Mr. Rice

Mike

Ann

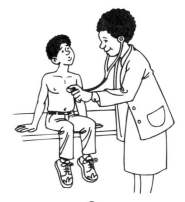

Sue

7. Ann _____ a gardener. She _____.

8. Mike _____ a gardener. He _____ an artist.

9. Jim _____ a bus driver. He _____.

10. Sue _____ a photographer. She _____.

11. Mr. Rice _____ a police officer. He isn't _____.

12. Ms. Black isn't _____. She _____.

	NOUN	+	*BE*	+	ADJECTIVE	
(a)	A ball		is		**round**.	*round*
(b)	Balls		are		**round.**	*intelligent*
(c)	Mary		is		**intelligent**.	*hungry* }= adjectives
(d)	Mary and Tom		are		**intelligent.**	*young*
						happy

	PRONOUN	+	*BE*	+	ADJECTIVE
(e)	I		am		**hungry**.
(f)	She		is		**young**.
(g)	They		are		**happy**.

Adjectives often follow a form of *be* (*am, is, are*). Adjectives describe or give information about a noun or pronoun that comes at the beginning of a sentence.★

★The noun or pronoun that comes at the beginning of a sentence is called a "subject." See Chart 4-1.

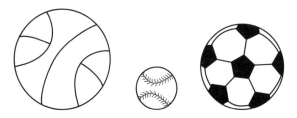

■ **EXERCISE 13:** Complete the drawings.

STUDENT A: Make the faces **happy**, **sad**, and **angry**. Show your drawings to Student B.

STUDENT B: Identify the emotions that Student A showed in the drawings. For example: *She is angry. He is sad. They are happy.*

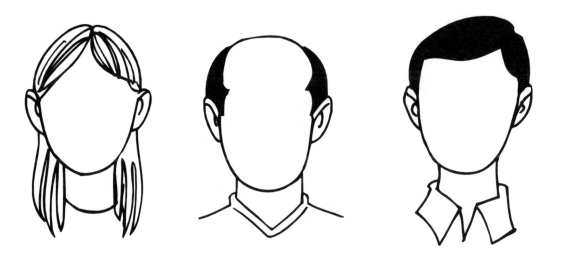

■ **EXERCISE 14:** Find the ADJECTIVE in the first sentence. Then complete the second sentence with **be** + an adjective that has an opposite meaning. Use the adjectives in the list. Use each adjective only one time.

beautiful	expensive	open
clean	fast	poor
cold	✔ happy	short
dangerous	noisy	sour
easy	old	tall

1. I'm not sad. I _'m happy_____.

2. Ice isn't hot. It _____.

3. Mr. Thomas isn't rich. He _____.

4. My hair isn't long. It _____.

5. My clothes aren't dirty. They _____.

6. Flowers aren't ugly. They _____.

7. Cars aren't cheap. They _____.

8. Airplanes aren't slow. They _____.

9. Grammar isn't difficult. It _____.

10. My sister isn't short. She _____.

11. My grandparents aren't young. They _____.

12. The dormitory isn't quiet. It _____.

13. The door isn't closed. It _____.

14. Guns aren't safe. They _____.

15. Lemons aren't sweet. They _____.

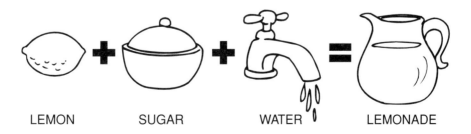

LEMON   SUGAR   WATER   LEMONADE

■ **EXERCISE 15—ORAL (BOOKS CLOSED):** Use ADJECTIVES to describe things in the classroom. Suggestions are given in parentheses.

Example: round, square, flat
To STUDENT A: *(The teacher writes the words on the board:* round, square, flat, *and then touches or points to something round, for example, a ring or a circle drawn on the board.)*
Tell me about this ring that I'm holding. Use one of the words on the board.
STUDENT A: It's round.
To STUDENT B: Tell me about this coin.
STUDENT B: It's round. It's flat.

1. round (a ring, a coin, a circle drawn on the board)
2. square (a box, a desk, a figure drawn on the board)
3. flat (a coin, a desktop)
4. full (a pocket, a hand)
5. empty (a pocket, a hand)
6. wet (a street on a rainy day, a licked finger)
7. dry (indoors on a rainy day, an unlicked finger)
8. dirty (a hand or a piece of paper rubbed on the floor)
9. clean (a hand or a piece of paper not rubbed on the floor)
10. long (a string, a strip of paper, someone's hair)
11. short (a string, a strip of paper, someone's hair)
12. heavy (a desk, a pile of books)
13. light (a piece of paper, a pen)
14. loud (a knock on a door or desk top, one's speaking voice)
15. soft (a knock on a door or desk top, one's speaking voice)
16. quiet (no sound at all in the classroom)

■ **EXERCISE 16:** Make sentences by using *is* or *are* and an ADJECTIVE from the following list. Use each adjective only one time.

beautiful	✔ *hot*	*sour*
cold	*important*	*square*
dry	*large/big*	*sweet*
flat	*round*	*wet*
funny	*small/little*	

1. Fire _____ *is hot* _____.

2. Ice and snow _____.

3. A box _____.

4. Balls and oranges _____.

5. Sugar _____.

6. An elephant _____,

    but a mouse _____.

7. A rain forest _____,

    but a desert _____.

8. A lemon _____.

9. A joke _____.

10. Good health _____.

11. Flowers _____.

12. A coin _____ small, round, and _____.

■ **EXERCISE 17:**   Complete the sentences. Use *is, isn't, are,* or *aren't.*

1. A ball _____*isn't*_____ square.

2. Balls _____*are*_____ round.

3. A mouse _____ big.

4. Lemons _____ yellow.

    Ripe bananas _____ yellow too.

5. A lemon _____ sweet. It _____ sour.

6. A diamond _____ cheap.

7. Diamonds _____ expensive.

8. Apples _____ expensive.

9. The earth _____ flat. It _____ round.

10. My pen _____ heavy. It _____ light.

11. This room _____ dark. It _____ light.

12. English grammar _____ hard. It _____ **easy.**

13. This exercise _____ difficult. It _____ **easy.**

14. My classmates _____ friendly.

15. A turtle _____ slow.

16. Airplanes _____ slow.

    They _____ fast.

17. The floor in the classroom _____ clean.

    It _____ dirty.

18. The weather _____ cold today.

19. The sun _____ bright today.

20. Ice cream and candy _____ sour. They _____ sweet.

21. My shoes _____ comfortable.

22. My desk _____ comfortable.

23. Flowers _____ ugly. They _____ beautiful.

24. Traffic at rush hour _____ noisy. It _____ quiet.

■ **EXERCISE 18—ORAL:** Do any of these words describe you?

    Example: Hungry?
    Response: I'm hungry. OR: I'm not hungry.

1. hungry?	11. angry?
2. thirsty?	12. nervous?
3. sleepy?	13. friendly?
4. tired?	14. lazy?
5. old?	15. hardworking?
6. young?	16. famous?
7. happy?	17. sick?
8. homesick?	18. healthy?
9. married?	19. friendly?
10. single?	20. shy?

■ **EXERCISE 19—ORAL:** Do any of these words describe this city?

1. big?
2. small?
3. old?
4. modern?
5. clean?

6. dirty?
7. friendly?
8. unfriendly?
9. safe?
10. dangerous?

■ **EXERCISE 20—ORAL (BOOKS CLOSED):** Make sentences. Use *is/isn't* or *are/aren't*.

Example: A ball \ round
Response: A ball is round.
Example: Balls \ square
Response: Balls aren't square.

1. A box \ square
2. A box \ round
3. The earth \ flat
4. The earth \ round
5. Bananas \ red
6. Bananas \ yellow
7. Diamonds \ expensive
8. Diamonds \ cheap
9. Apples \ expensive
10. Air \ free
11. Cars \ free
12. A pen \ heavy
13. A pen \ light
14. Flowers \ ugly
15. A rose \ beautiful
16. A turtle \ fast

17. A turtle \ slow
18. Airplanes \ slow
19. Airplanes \ fast
20. English grammar \ difficult
21. English grammar \ easy
22. This exercise \ hard
23. The weather \ hot today
24. The weather \ cold today
25. Lemons \ sweet
26. Ice cream and candy \ sour
27. Traffic \ noisy
28. City streets \ quiet
29. Education \ important
30. Good food \ important
31. Good food and exercise \ important
32. The students in this class \ very intelligent

■ **EXERCISE 21—ORAL (BOOKS CLOSED):** Name things that the given ADJECTIVES can describe.

Example: round
TEACHER: Name something that is round.
STUDENT: (A ball, an orange, the world, my head, etc.) is round.

1. hot
2. square
3. sweet
4. sour
5. large

6. flat
7. little
8. important
9. cold
10. funny

11. beautiful
12. expensive
13. cheap
14. free
15. delicious

(a) Maria is **here**. (b) Bob was **at the library**.	In (a): *here* = a location. In (b): *at the library* = a location. **Be** is often followed by *a location*.	

(c) Maria is	here. there. downstairs. upstairs. inside. outside. downtown.	A location may be one word, as in the examples in (c).

	PREPOSITION + NOUN	A location may be a prepositional phrase, as in (d). *A preposition + a noun* is called a "prepositional phrase." *At the library* = a prepositional phrase.
(d) Bob was	*at* **the library**. *on* **the bus**. *in* **his room**. *at* **work**. *next to* **Maria**.	

SOME COMMON PREPOSITIONS

above	*between*	*next to*
at	*from*	*on*
behind	*in*	*under*

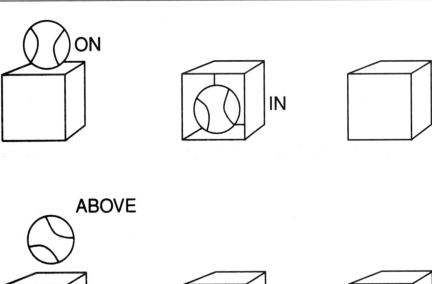

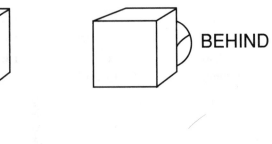

■ **EXERCISE 22:** Complete the sentences with PREPOSITIONS that describe the pictures. Use each preposition one time.

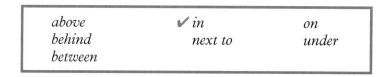

above	✔ in	on
behind	next to	under
between		

1.

The cat is _____*in*_____ the desk.

2.

The cat is _____ the desk.

3.

The cat is _____ the desk.

4.

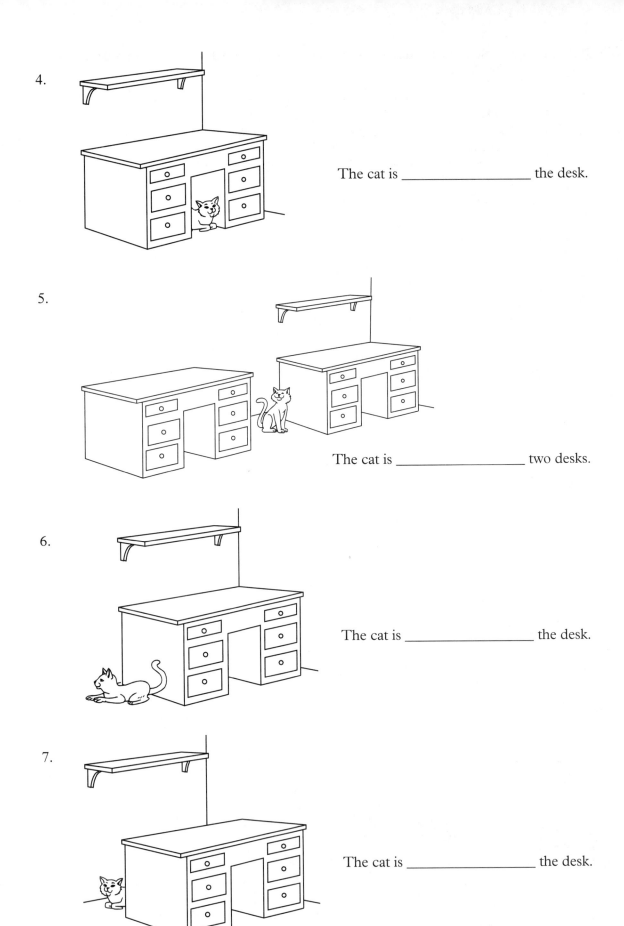

The cat is _____ the desk.

5.

The cat is _____ two desks.

6.

The cat is _____ the desk.

7.

The cat is _____ the desk.

■ **EXERCISE 23:**   Find the PREPOSITIONS and the PREPOSITIONAL PHRASES in the following
sentences.

    1. Mike is in his apartment.
       → *in = a preposition*
       → *in his apartment = a prepositional phrase*

    2. Mr. Lee is at the airport.

    3. Ali is from Egypt.

    4. My book is on my desk.

    5. Bob's pen is in his pocket.

    6. The post office is on First Street.

    7. The post office is next to the bank.

    8. My feet are under my desktop.

    9. My nose is between my cheeks.

    10. My apartment is on the third floor. It is above Mr. Kwan's apartment.

■ **EXERCISE 24—ORAL (BOOKS CLOSED):**   Practice using PREPOSITIONS of location.

Example:	under	
TEACHER	Put your hand under your chair. Where is your hand?	
STUDENT:	My hand is under my chair. / It's under my chair.	

    1. *on*   Put your pen on your book. Where is your pen?
    2. *in*   Put your pen in your book. Where's your pen?
    3. *under*   Put your pen under your book. Where's your pen?
    4. *next to*   Put your pen next to your book. Where's your pen?
    5. *on*   Put your hand on your ear. Where's your hand?
    6. *next to*   Put your hand next to your ear. Where's your hand?
    7. *above*   Put your hand above your head. Where's your hand?
    8. *next to*   Stand next to (. . .). Where are you?
    9. *between* Stand between (. . .) and (. . .). Where are you?
   10. *between* Put your pen between two books. Where's your pen?
   11. *behind*   Put your hand behind your head. Where's your hand?
   12. Follow these directions: Put your pen   in your hand.
                          . . . on your arm.
                          . . . behind your neck.
                          . . . between your hands.
                          . . . under your book.
                          . . . next to your book.
                          . . . above your book.

1-8 SUMMARY: SENTENCE PATTERNS WITH *BE*

(a) SUBJECT + *BE* + NOUN I am *a student.*	The noun or pronoun that comes at the beginning of a sentence is called the "subject."
(b) SUBJECT + *BE* + ADJECTIVE He is *intelligent.*	***Be*** is a "verb." Almost all English sentences have a subject and a verb.
(c) SUBJECT + *BE* + A LOCATION We are *in class.*	Notice in the examples: There are three basic completions for sentences that begin with a *subject + the verb **be***: • *a noun*, as in (a) • *an adjective*, as in (b) • *an expression of location*, as in (c)

■ **EXERCISE 25:** Write the form of *be (**am**, **is**, or **are**)* that is used in each sentence. Then write the grammar structure that follows *be*.

		BE	+	COMPLETION
1. We're students.	→	are	+	N *(a noun)*
2. Anna is in Rome.	→	is	+	LOC *(a location)*
3. I'm hungry.	→	am	+	ADJ *(an adjective)*
4. Dogs are animals.	→	_____	+	_____
5. Jack is at home.	→	_____	+	_____
6. He's sick.	→	_____	+	_____
7. They're artists.	→	_____	+	_____
8. I'm in class.	→	_____	+	_____
9. Gina is upstairs.	→	_____	+	_____
10. My pockets are empty.	→	_____	+	_____

■ **EXERCISE 26—ORAL:** *Is* and *are* are often contracted with nouns in spoken English. Listen to your teacher say the contractions in the following sentences and practice saying them yourself.

1. Grammar is easy.
   ("Grammar's easy.")

2. Rita is a student.

3. My book is on the table.

4. My books are on the table.

5. The weather is cold today.

6. My brother is twenty-one years old.

7. The window is open.

8. The windows are open.

9. My money is in my wallet.

10. Mr. Smith is a teacher.

11. Tom is at home now.

12. The sun is bright today.

13. My roommate is from Chicago.

14. My roommates are from Chicago.

15. My sister is a student in high school.

1-9 YES/NO QUESTIONS WITH *BE*

QUESTION	STATEMENT	In a question, ***be*** comes in front of the subject.
BE + SUBJECT (a) ***Is*** **she** a student? (b) ***Are*** **they** at home?	SUBJECT + *BE* **She** **is** a student. **They** **are** at home.	*Punctuation:* A question ends with a question mark (?). A statement ends with a period (.).

When people answer a question, they usually give only a "short answer" (but sometimes they give a "long answer" too). Notice in the short answers below:
    After yes, ***be*** is not contracted with a pronoun.★
    After *no*, two contractions of ***be*** are possible with no differences in meaning.

QUESTION	SHORT ANSWER + (LONG ANSWER)		
(c) ***Is she*** a student?	→	Yes, ***she is.***★	(She's a student.)
	→	No, ***she's not.***	(She's not a student.) OR:
	→	No, ***she isn't***.	(She isn't a student.)
(d) ***Are they*** at home?	→	Yes, ***they are.***★	(They're at home.)
	→	No, ***they're not.***	(They're not at home.) OR:
	→	No, ***they aren't***.	(They aren't at home.)

★ INCORRECT: *Yes, she's.*
  INCORRECT: *Yes, they're.*

■ **EXERCISE 27:**   Make questions and give short answers.

1. A: _____*Are you tired?*_____

   B: _____*No, I'm not.*_____ (I'm not tired.)

2. A: _____*Is Anna in your class?*_____

   B: _____*Yes, she is.*_____ (Anna is in my class.)

3. A: _____

   B: _____ (I'm not homesick.)

4. A: _____

   B: _____ (Bob is homesick.)

5. A: _____

   B: _____ (Sue isn't here today.)

6. A: _____

   B: _____ (The students in this class are intelligent.)

7. A: _____

   B: _____ (The chairs in this room aren't comfortable.)

8. A: _____

   B: _____ (I'm not married.)

9. A: _____

   B: _____ (Tom and I are roommates.)

10. A: _____

    B: _____ (A butterfly is not a bird.)

■ **EXERCISE 28—ORAL (BOOKS CLOSED):** Ask and answer questions.

STUDENT A: Your book is open. Ask a classmate a question. Use "**_Are you . . . ?_**"
STUDENT B: Your book is closed. Answer Student A's question.
Example: hungry
STUDENT A: (Yoko), are you hungry?
STUDENT B: Yes, I am.   OR: No, I'm not.

1. hungry
2. sleepy
3. thirsty
4. married
5. single
6. tired
7. homesick
8. lazy
9. cold
10. comfortable
11. a student
12. a teacher
13. a famous actor
14. in the middle of the room

Switch roles.
15. in the back of the room
16. in the front of the room
17. in class
18. in bed
19. at the library
20. at home
21. in _(name of this city)_
22. in _(name of another city)_
23. in Canada
24. in the United States
25. from the United States
26. from _(name of country)_
27. a student at _(name of school)_

■ **EXERCISE 29—ORAL (BOOKS CLOSED):** Ask a classmate a question.

STUDENT A: Your book is open. Ask a classmate a question. Use "**_Are you . . . ?_**"
STUDENT B: Your book is closed. Answer Student A's question.
Example: a ball \ round
STUDENT A: (. . .), is a ball round?
STUDENT B: Yes, it is.
Example: a ball \ square
STUDENT A: (. . .), is a ball square?
STUDENT B: No, it isn't.   OR: No, it's not.

1. a mouse \ big
2. sugar \ sweet
3. lemons \ sweet
4. ice cream and candy \ sour
5. the world \ flat
6. the world \ round
7. your desk \ comfortable
8. your shoes \ comfortable
9. your eyes \ brown
10. the sun \ bright today
11. the weather \ cold today

Switch roles.
12. your pen \ heavy
13. apples \ expensive
14. diamonds \ cheap
15. English grammar \ easy
16. the floor in this room \ clean
17. butterflies \ beautiful
18. turtles \ intelligent
19. your dictionary \ under your desk
20. your books \ on your desk
21. your desk \ in the middle of the room
22. your pen \ in your pocket

1-10 QUESTIONS WITH *BE*: USING *WHERE*

Where asks about location. *Where* comes at the beginning of the question, in front of *be*.

QUESTION	SHORT ANSWER + (LONG ANSWER)

	BE + SUBJECT		
(a)	*Is*	*the book* on the table?	→ Yes, *it is.* (The book is on the table.)
(b)	*Are*	*the books* on the table?	→ Yes, *they are.* (The books are on the table.)

	WHERE + *BE* + SUBJECT			
(c)	*Where*	*is*	*the book?*	→ *On the table.* (The book is on the table.)
(d)	*Where*	*are*	*the books?*	→ *On the table.* (The books are on the table.)

■ **EXERCISE 30:** Make questions.

1. A: _____ *Is Kate at home?* _____
   B: Yes, she is. (Kate is at home.)

2. A: _____ *Where is Kate?* _____
   B: At home. (Kate is at home.)

3. A: _____
   B: Yes, it is. (Cairo is in Egypt.)

4. A: _____
   B: In Egypt. (Cairo is in Egypt.)

5. A: _____
   B: Yes, they are. (The students are in class today.)

6. A: _____
   B: In class. (The students are in class today.)

7. A: _____
   B: On Main Street. (The post office is on Main Street.)

8. A: _____
   B: Yes, it is. (The train station is on Grand Avenue.)

9. A: _____
   B: Over there. (The bus stop is over there.)

10. A: _____
    B: At the zoo. (Sue and Ken are at the zoo today.)

■ **EXERCISE 31—ORAL (BOOKS CLOSED):** Ask a classmate a question. Use **where.**

Example: your pen
STUDENT A: Where is your pen?
STUDENT B: *(free response)*

1. your grammar book
2. your dictionary
3. your money
4. your books
5. (. . .)

6. (. . .) and (. . .)
7. your sunglasses
8. your pen
9. your apartment

10. your parents
11. the post office
12. *(the names of places in this city: a store, landmark, restaurant, etc.)*

■ **EXERCISE 32—ORAL:** Ask and answer questions using **where** and the map of North America.

Example: Washington, D.C.
STUDENT A: Where's Washington, D.C.?
STUDENT B: *(Pointing at the map)* It's here.

Suggestions:
1. New York City
2. Los Angeles
3. Montreal
4. Miami
5. Toronto
6. Washington, D. C.
7. the Great Lakes
8. the Rocky Mountains
9. the Mississippi River
10. Mexico City

Washington, D.C.

1-11 USING *HAVE* AND *HAS*

	SINGULAR		PLURAL			
(a)	*I* **have** a pen.	(f)	*We* **have** pens.	*I* *you* *we* *they*	}	+ **have**
(b)	*You* **have** a pen.	(g)	*You* **have** pens.			
(c)	*She* **has** a pen.	(h)	*They* **have** pens.			
(d)	*He* **has** a pen.			*she* *he* *it*	}	+ **has**
(e)	*It* **has** blue ink.					

■ **EXERCISE 33:** Complete the sentences. Use **have** and **has.**

1. We _____*have*_____ grammar books.

2. I _____ a dictionary.

3. Kate _____ a blue pen. She _____ a blue notebook too.

4. You _____ a pen in your pocket.

5. Bob _____ a notebook on his desk.

6. Anna and Bob _____ notebooks. They _____ pens too.

7. Samir is a student in our class. He _____ a red grammar book.

8. I _____ a grammar book. It _____ a red cover.

9. You and I are students. We _____ books on our desks.

10. Mike _____ a wallet in his pocket. Sara _____ a wallet in her purse.

11. Nadia isn't in class today because she _____ the flu.

12. Mr. and Mrs. Johnson _____ two daughters.

1-12 USING *MY, YOUR, HIS, HER, OUR, THEIR*

	SINGULAR		PLURAL

	SINGULAR			PLURAL
(a)	**I** have a book. ***My*** book is red.		(e)	**We** have books. ***Our*** books are red.
(b)	**You** have a book. ***Your*** book is red.		(f)	**You** have books. ***Your*** books are red.
(c)	**She** has a book. ***Her*** book is red.		(g)	**They** have books. ***Their*** books are red.
(d)	**He** has a book. ***His*** book is red.			

SUBJECT FORM		POSSESSIVE FORM
I	→	*my*
you	→	*your*
she	→	*her*
he	→	*his*
we	→	*our*
they	→	*their*

I *possess* a book. = I *have* a book. = It is *my* book.

My, our, her, his, our, and *their* are called "possessive adjectives." They come in front of nouns.

■ **EXERCISE 34:**   Complete the sentences. Use ***my***, ***your***, ***his***, ***her***, ***our***, or ***their***.

1. I have a pen. _____*My*_____ pen is blue.

2. You have a pen. _____ pen is black.

3. Kate has a pen. _____ pen is green.

4. Jim has a pen. _____ pen is yellow.

5. Sara and I have pens. _____ pens are gray.

6. Sara and you have pens. _____ pens are red.

7. Sam and Kate have pens. _____ pens are orange.

8. I have a sister. _____ sister is twenty-one years old.

9. Ann has a car. _____ car is a Ford.

10. You have a pen. _____ pen is a ballpoint.

11. Jim and you have mustaches. _____ mustaches are dark.

12. Ann and Alex have a baby. _____ baby is eight months old.

13. Alice and I have notebooks. _____ notebooks are green.

14. Ann has a brother. _____ brother is in high school.

15. Ken has a coat. _____ coat is brown.

16. We have a dog. _____ dog is gray and white.

■ **EXERCISE 35:** Complete the sentences. Use **have** or **has**. Use **my, your, her, his, our,** or **their**.

1. I _____*have*_____ a book. _____*My*_____ book is interesting.

2. Bob _____ a bookbag. _____ bookbag is green.

3. You _____ a raincoat. _____ raincoat is brown.

4. Kate _____ a raincoat. _____ raincoat is red.

5. Ann and Jim are married. They _____ a baby. _____ baby is six months old.

6. Ken and Sue _____ a daughter. _____ daughter is ten years old.

7. John and I _____ a son. _____ son is seven years old.

8. I _____ a brother. _____ brother is sixteen.

9. We _____ grammar books. _____ grammar books are red.

10. Tom and you _____ bookbags. _____ bookbags are green.

11. Ann _____ a dictionary. _____ dictionary is red.

12. Mike _____ a car. _____ car is blue.

■ **EXERCISE 36:** Complete the sentences with **my, your, her, his, our,** or **their**.

1. Rita is wearing a blouse. _____ blouse is light blue.

2. Tom is wearing a shirt. _____ shirt is yellow and brown.

3. I am wearing jeans. _____ jeans are blue.

4. Bob and Tom are wearing boots. _____ boots are brown.

5. Sue and you are wearing dresses. _____ dresses are red.

6. Ann and I are wearing sweaters. _____ sweaters are green.

7. You are wearing shoes. _____ shoes are dark brown.

8. Sue is wearing a skirt. _____ skirt is black.

9. John is wearing a belt. _____ belt is white.

10. Sue and Ann are wearing slacks. _____ slacks are dark gray.

11. Tom is wearing slacks. _____ slacks are dark blue.

12. I am wearing earrings. _____ earrings are gold.

VOCABULARY CHECKLIST

COLORS	CLOTHES	JEWELRY
black	belt	bracelet
blue, dark blue, light blue	blouse	earrings
blue green	boots	necklace
brown, dark brown, light brown	coat	ring
gray, dark gray, light gray	dress	watch/wristwatch
green, dark green, light green	gloves	
orange	hat	
pink	jacket	
purple	jeans	
red	pants	
tan, beige	sandals	
white	shirt	
yellow	shoes	
gold	skirt	
silver	slacks	
	suit	
	sweater	
	tie, necktie	
	T-shirt	

■ **EXERCISE 37—ORAL (BOOKS CLOSED):** Name some of the colors and then some of the articles of clothing and jewelry in the room. Then describe an article of clothing/jewelry and its color, using this pattern:

*possessive adjective + noun + **is/are** + color*

Examples:

TEACHER: Look at Ali. Tell me about his shirt. What color is his shirt?
STUDENT: His shirt is blue.

TEACHER: Look at Rosa. What is this?
STUDENT: A sweater.
TEACHER: Tell me about her sweater. What color is it?
STUDENT: Her sweater is red.

TEACHER: Look at me. What am I touching?
STUDENT: Your shoes.
TEACHER: Tell me about the color.
STUDENT: Your shoes are brown.

1-13 USING *THIS* AND *THAT*

(a) I have a book in my hand. **This book** is red. (b) I see a book on your desk. **That book** is blue. (c) **This** is my book. (d) **That** is your book.	*this* book = the book is near me. *that* book = the book is not near me.
(e) **That's** her book.	CONTRACTION: *that is = that's*

THIS BOOK

THAT BOOK

■ **EXERCISE 38—ORAL (BOOKS CLOSED):** Use *this* and *that*. Touch and point to things in the classroom.

Example: book
Response: This is my book. That is your book.

1. book	5. dictionary	9. pencil
2. pen	6. bookbag	10. pencil sharpener
3. notebook	7. coat	11. watch
4. purse	8. hat	12. nose

■ **EXERCISE 39—ORAL (BOOKS CLOSED):** Use *this* and *that*. Touch and point to things in the classroom.

Example: red \ yellow
Response: This (book) is red. That (shirt) is yellow.

1. red \ blue	7. red \ pink
2. red \ green	8. dark blue \ light blue
3. red \ yellow	9. black \ gray
4. blue \ black	10. gold \ silver
5. white \ black	11. dark brown \ tan
6. orange \ green	12. purple \ red

1-14 USING *THESE* AND *THOSE*

	SINGULAR		PLURAL
(a) My books are on my desk. **These** are my books.	*this*	→	*these*
(b) Your books are on your desk. **Those** are your books.	*that*	→	*those*

■ **EXERCISE 40:**   Complete the sentences. Use the words in parentheses.

1. *(This, These)* _____*These*_____ books belong to me. *(That, Those)*

    _____*That*_____ book belongs to Kate.

2. *(This, These)* _____ coat is black. *(That, Those)* _____

    coats are tan.

3. *(This, These)* _____ earrings are gold. *(That, Those)* _____

    earrings are silver.

4. *(This, These)* _____ pencil belongs to Alex. *(That, Those)*

    _____ pencil belongs to Alice.

5. *(This, These)* _____ sunglasses belong to me. *(That, Those)*

    _____ sunglasses belong to you.

6. *(This, These)* _____ exercise is easy. *(That, Those)* _____

    exercises are hard.

7. Students are sitting at *(this, these)* _____ desks, but *(that, those)*

    _____ desks are empty.

8. *(This, These)* _____ book is on my desk. *(That, Those)*

    _____ books are on your desk.

■ **EXERCISE 41—ORAL (BOOKS CLOSED):**   Use *these* and *those*. Touch and point to
   things in the classroom.

   Example: books
   Response: These are my books. Those are your books.

   1. books   5. jeans
   2. pens   6. things
   3. shoes   7. glasses/sunglasses
   4. earrings   8. notebooks

■ **EXERCISE 42—ORAL (BOOKS CLOSED):** Use *this*, *that*, *these*, or *those*. Touch and point to things in the classroom.

Example: book
Response: This is my book. That is your book.
Example: books
Response: These are my books. Those are your books.

1. book	6. coats
2. books	7. shoes
3. dictionary	8. wallet
4. pens	9. purse
5. pen	10. glasses

1-15 ASKING QUESTIONS WITH *WHAT* AND *WHO* + *BE*

(a) **What is** this (thing)? → It's a pen. (b) **Who is** that (man)? → That's Mr. Lee. (c) **What are** those (things)? → They're pens. (d) **Who are** they? → They're Mr. and Mrs. Lee.	**What** asks about things. **Who** asks about people. NOTE: In questions with **what** and **who**, • **is** is followed by a singular word. • **are** is followed by a plural word.
(e) **What's** this? (f) **Who's** that man?	CONTRACTIONS *who is = who's* *what is = what's*

■ **EXERCISE 43:** Complete the questions with *what* or *who* and *is* or *are*.

1. A: ____*Who is*_____ that woman?
   B: She's my sister. Her name is Sonya.

2. A: _____ those things?
   B: They're ballpoint pens.

3. A: _____ that?
   B: That's Ms. Walenski.

4. A: _____ this?
   B: That's my new notebook.

5. A: Look at those people over there. _____ they?
   B: I'm not sure, but I think they're new students from Thailand.

6. A: _____ your name?
   B: Anita.

7. A: _____ your grammar teacher?
   B: Mr. Cook.

8. A: _____ your favorite teachers?
   B: Mr. Cook and Ms. Rosenberg.

9. A: _____ a rabbit?
   B: It's a small furry animal with big ears.

10. A: _____ bats?
    B: They're animals that can fly. They're not birds.

■ **EXERCISE 45—ORAL:** Talk about things and people in the classroom. Ask your classmates the given questions.

Example: What's this?
STUDENT A: What's this? *(pointing at his/her grammar book)*
STUDENT B: It's your grammar book.
Example: Who's that?
STUDENT A: Who's that? *(indicating a classmate)*
STUDENT B: That's Ivan.

1. What's this?
2. What's that?
3. Who's this?
4. Who's that?
5. What are those?
6. What are these?

■ **EXERCISE 46:** Study the names of the parts of the body in Picture A. Then cover Picture A and write in the names of the body parts in Picture B.

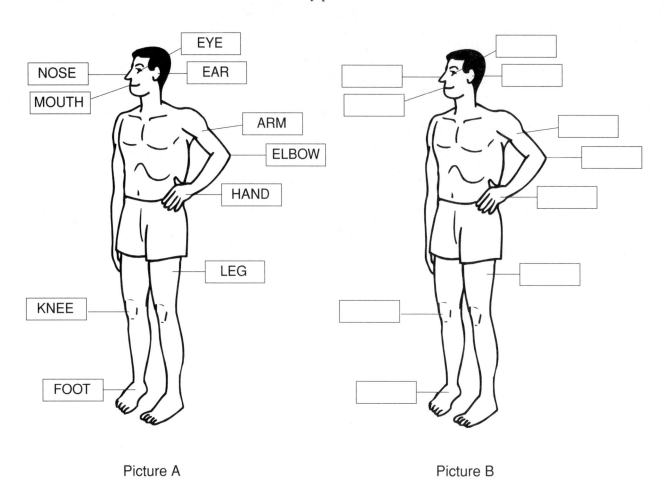

Picture A   Picture B

■ **EXERCISE 47—ORAL (BOOKS CLOSED):** Use *this*, *that*, *these*, and *those*.

> *Example:* hand
> TEACHER: What is this? *(The teacher indicates her or his hand.)*
> STUDENT: That is your hand.
>
>   OR
>
> TEACHER: What is that? *(The teacher indicates a student's hand.)*
> STUDENT: This is my hand.

1. nose
2. eyes
3. arm
4. elbow
5. legs

6. knee
7. foot
8. shoulder
9. fingers
10. ears

■ **EXERCISE 48—ORAL:** Ask a classmate questions about the picture. Use **What's this?** **What's that?** **What are these?** **What are those?** and any other questions you want to ask.

Example:
STUDENT A: What's this? *(pointing at the tree)*
STUDENT B: That's a tree.
STUDENT A: What are those? *(pointing at the horses)*
STUDENT B: Those are horses.
Etc.

■ **EXERCISE 49:** Draw a picture and then answer a classmate's question about it. Use **What's this? What's that? What are these? What are those?** and any other questions you want to ask.

Suggestions for the picture you draw:
1. this classroom
2. some of the people in this classroom
3. your family
4. your room / apartment / house
5. a scene at a zoo
6. an outdoor scene

■ **EXERCISE 50—REVIEW:** Underline the NOUNS, ADJECTIVES, PRONOUNS, POSSESSIVE ADJECTIVES, and PREPOSITIONAL PHRASES.

PART I: Find the NOUNS and ADJECTIVES.

    noun   *adj.*
1. <u>Balls</u> are <u>round</u>.

2. Flowers are beautiful.

3. Birds have wings.

4. Bats aren't birds.

5. Bats aren't blind.

PART II: Find the PRONOUNS and POSSESSIVE ADJECTIVES.

               pronoun   *poss. adj.*
6. Bats have wings, but <u>they</u> aren't birds. Bats use <u>their</u> wings to fly.

7. I have a grammar book. It's red. My dictionary is red too.

8. My book is red, and your book is red too.

9. An egg isn't square. It's oval.

10. Tina has three sons. She is at home today. They are at school. Her sons are good

students.

PART III: Find the PREPOSITIONAL PHRASES.

             prep. phr.
11. Libya is <u>in Africa</u>.

12. Po is from Beijing.

13. My books are on my desk.

14. I'm at school.

15. My middle finger is between my index finger and my ring finger.

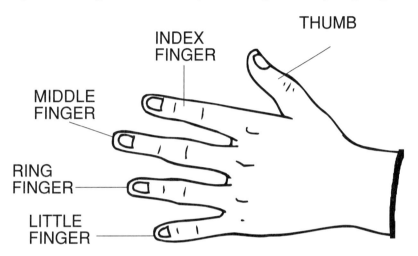

■ **EXERCISE 51—REVIEW:** Correct the mistakes in the sentences.

       are
1. We ~~is~~ students.

2. I no hungry.

3. I am student. He is teacher.

4. Yoko not here. She at school.

5. I'm from Mexico. Where you are from?

6. Roberto he is a student in your class?

7. Those pictures are beautifuls.

8. This is you dictionary. It not my dictionary.

9. Mr. Lee have a brown coat.

10. They are n't here today.

11. This books are expensive.

12. Cuba is a island.

13. Florida and Korea is peninsula.

■ **EXERCISE 52—REVIEW:**   Choose the correct completion.

Example:

Those _____*B*_____ expensive.
    A.   book is   B.   books are   C. books is

1. Ann _____ a grammar book.
    A.   have   B.   is   C. has

2. This floor _____.
    A.   dirty is   B.   dirty   C. is dirty

3. _____ yellow.
    A.   A banana are   B.   A banana is   C. Bananas is

4. *Bob:*   _____ is your apartment?
   Ann: It's on Forest Street.
    A.   What   B.   Where   C. Who

5. Mike is _____ engineer.
    A.   a   B.   an   C. on

6. Give this to Ann. It is _____ dictionary.
    A.   she   B.   an   C. her

7. *Yoko:*   _____ these?
   Gina: My art books. I'm taking an art history course this semester.
    A.   What is   B.   Who are   C. What are

8. *Tom:* Are you hungry?

   Sue: Yes, _____.
    A.   I'm   B.   I'm not   C. I am

9. _____ books are really expensive.
    A.   Those   B.   They   C. This

10. *Tina:* _____ that?
    Jim: That's Paul Carter.
      A. Who's   B. What's   C. Where's

11. That is _____.
      A. a mistakes   B. mistakes   C. a mistake

12. *Paul:* _____ in your class?
    Eric: No.
      A. Mr. Kim   B. Is Mr. Kim   C. Mr. Kim is he

■ **EXERCISE 53—REVIEW:** Complete the sentences with *am*, *is*, or *are*. Use *not* if necessary.

1. Lemons _____ vegetables.

2. A lemon _____ a kind of fruit.

3. I _____ from the United States.

4. We _____ human beings.

5. Eggs _____ oval.

6. Chickens _____ birds, but bats _____ birds.

7. Salt _____ sweet. Sugar _____ sweet.

8. Soccer _____ a sport.

9. Soccer and basketball _____ sports.

10. Africa _____ a country. It _____ a continent.

■ **EXERCISE 54—REVIEW:** Complete the sentences.

1. A: _____*Are*_____ you a student at this school?

   B: Yes, _____.

   A: Where _____ you from?

   B: I _____ Korea.

2. A: Where _____ your book?

   B: Yoko _____ it.

   A: Where _____ your notebooks?

   B: Ali and Roberto _____ my notebooks.

3. A: _____ this?

   B: It _____ picture of my family.

   A: _____ this?

   B: That's _____ father.

   A: _____ they?
   B: My brother and sister.

4. A: Are you a _____?

   B: No, _____ not. I'm a _____.

5. A: Are _____ expensive?

   B: Yes, _____.

   A: Is _____ expensive?

   B: No, _____.

6. A: What's _____?
   B: I don't know. Ask someone else.

   A: What's _____?

   B: It's _____.

7. A: _____ an animal?
   B: Yes.

   A: _____ animals?
   B: Yes.

   A: _____ an insect?
   B: No, it's not. It's an animal too.

8. A: _____ countries in Asia?
   B: Yes, they are.

   A: _____ a country in South America?
   B: Yes, it is.

   A: _____ a country in Africa?

   B: No, it's not. It's a country in _____.

9. A: Where _____?

   B: He's _____.

   A: Where _____?

   B: They're _____.

10. A: _____ a turtle?
     B: Just a minute. Let me look in my dictionary. Okay. A turtle is a reptile.

     A: _____ a reptile?

     B: _____ an animal that has cold blood.

     A: _____ snakes reptiles too?

     B: Yes. _____ reptiles too.

■ **EXERCISE 55—REVIEW:** Work in pairs.

STUDENT A: Give directions. Your book is open.
STUDENT B: Draw what Student A tells you to draw. Your book is closed.

1. Draw a ball on a box.
2. Draw a ball above a box.
3. Draw a ball next to a box.
4. Draw a ball under a box.
5. Draw a ball in a box.
6. Draw a banana between two apples.
7. Draw a square above a circle.
8. Draw a flower. Draw a tree next to the flower. Draw a bird above the tree. Draw a turtle under the flower.

Switch roles.
9. Draw a circle next to a triangle.
10. Draw a circle in a triangle.
11. Draw a circle above a triangle.
12. Draw a triangle between two circles.
13. Draw a circle under a triangle.
14. Draw an apple on a banana. Draw an apple above a banana.
15. Draw a tree. Draw a person next to the tree. Draw the sun above the tree.
16. Draw a cloud. Draw a bird under the cloud. Draw a bird above the cloud. Draw a bird in the cloud.

■ **EXERCISE 56—REVIEW:** Work in pairs.

> STUDENT A: Give directions. Use the given prepositions.
> STUDENT B: Perform the action.

> *Example:* in
> STUDENT A: Put your pen in your pocket.
> STUDENT B: *(Student B puts her/his pen in her/his pocket.)*

Switch roles.

1. in	8. in
2. on	9. between
3. above	10. behind
4. under	11. above
5. between	12. on
6. next to	13. next to
7. behind	14. under

■ **EXERCISE 57—REVIEW:** Complete the sentences in this composition by Carlos.

(1) My name ____*is*____ Carlos. ____*I am* OR *I'm*____ from Mexico.

(2) _____ a student. _____ twenty years old.

(3) My family lives in Mexico City. _____ father _____ a

(4) businessman. _____ fifty-one years old. _____ mother

(5) _____ a housewife. _____ forty-nine years old.

(6) I _____ two sisters and one brother. The names of my sisters

(7) _____ Rosa and Patricia. Rosa _____ a teacher.

(8) _____ twenty-eight years old. Patricia _____ a student.

(9) _____ eighteen years old. The name of _____ brother

(10) _____ Pedro. _____ an engineer. He is married. He

(11) _____ two children.

(12) I live in a dormitory. _____ a tall building. _____ on

(13) Pine Street. My address _____ 3225 Pine St. I live with my roommate.

(14) _____ name is Bob. _____ from Chicago.

(15) _____ nineteen years old.

(16) I like my classes. _____ interesting. I like _____

(17) classmates. _____ friendly.

■ **EXERCISE 58—REVIEW:** Write a composition by completing the sentences. (Use your own paper.) NOTE: A sentence begins with a capital letter (a big letter) and a sentence ends with a period (.)★

My name _____. I _____ from _____. _____ a student. _____ years old.

My family lives in _____. _____ father _____ years old. _____ mother _____ years old.

I have _____ sister(s) and _____ brother(s). The name(s) of my sister(s) _____. _____ is a/an _____. _____ years old. *(Write about each sister.)* The name(s) of my brother(s) _____. _____ is a _____. _____ years old. *(Write about each brother.)*

I live in *(a dormitory, a house, an apartment)* _____. My address _____. I live with _____. _____ name(s) _____.

I like _____ classes. _____ are _____ and _____. I like _____ classmates. They _____.

_____
★In British English, a period is called a "full stop."

CHAPTER **2**
Expressing Present Time (Part 1)

2-1 FORM AND BASIC MEANING OF THE SIMPLE PRESENT TENSE

	SINGULAR	PLURAL
1st PERSON	**I talk**	**we talk**
2nd PERSON	**you talk**	**you talk**
3rd PERSON	**she talks**	**they talk**
	he talks	
	it rains	

Notice: The verb after **she, he, it** (3rd person singular) has a final **-s**: *talks.*

(a) I *eat* breakfast **every morning**.
(b) Ann *speaks* English **every day**.
(c) We *sleep* every night.
(d) They *go* to the beach **every weekend**.

The simple present tense expresses habits. In (a): Eating breakfast is a habit, a usual activity. *Every morning* = Monday morning, Tuesday morning, Wednesday morning, Thursday morning, Friday morning, Saturday morning, and Sunday morning.

■ **EXERCISE 1:** What do you do every morning? On the left, there is a list of habits. On the right, make a list of your habits every morning. Put them in order. What do you do first, second, third, etc.?

HABITS

(a) eat breakfast

(b) go to class

(c) put on my clothes

(d) drink a cup of coffee/tea

(e) shave

(f) put on my make-up

(g) take a shower/bath

(h) get up

(i) pick up my books

(j) walk to the bathroom

(k) watch TV

(l) look in the mirror

✔ (m) turn off the alarm clock

(n) go to the kitchen/the cafeteria

(o) brush/comb my hair

(p) say good-bye to my roommate/

     wife/husband

(q) brush my teeth

(r) do exercises

(s) wash my face

(t) stretch, yawn, and rub my eyes

(u) *other habits*

MY HABITS EVERY MORNING

1. *The alarm clock rings.*

2. ___ *I turn off the alarm clock.* ___

3. _____

4. _____

5. _____

6. _____

7. _____

8. _____

9. _____

10. _____

11. _____

12. _____

13. _____

14. _____

15. _____

16. _____

17. _____

18. _____

19. _____

20. _____

21. _____

22. _____

always	*usually*	*often*	*sometimes*	*seldom*	*rarely*	*never*
100%	99%–90%	90%–75%	75%–25%	25%–10%	10%–1%	0%

	SUBJECT +	FREQUENCY ADVERB +	SIMPLE PRESENT VERB	*Always, usually, often, sometimes, seldom, rarely* and *never* are called "frequency adverbs." They come between the subject and the simple present verb.★
(a)	**Bob**	*always*	*comes* to class.	
(b)	**Mary**	*usually*	*comes* to class.	
(c)	**We**	*often*	*watch* TV at night.	$$\text{SUBJECT} + \left\{\begin{array}{l}\text{always}\\ \text{usually}\\ \text{often}\\ \text{sometimes}\\ \text{seldom}\\ \text{rarely}\\ \text{never}\end{array}\right\} + \text{VERB}$$
(d)	**I**	*sometimes*	*drink* tea with dinner.	
(e)	**They**	*seldom*	*go* to the movies.	
(f)	**Anna**	*rarely*	*makes* a mistake.	
(g)	**I**	*never*	*eat* paper.	

★Some frequency adverbs can also come at the beginning or at the end of a sentence. For example:
Sometimes *I get up at seven.*   *I* **sometimes** *get up at seven.*   *I get up at seven* **sometimes.**
Also: See Chart 2-3 for the use of frequency adverbs with **be**.

	Sun.	Mon.	Tues.	Wed.	Thurs.	Fri.	Sat.
Ann **always** drinks tea with lunch.	☕	☕	☕	☕	☕	☕	☕
Bob **usually** drinks tea with lunch.		☕	☕	☕	☕	☕	☕
Maria **often** drinks tea with lunch.			☕	☕	☕	☕	☕
Gary **sometimes** drinks tea with lunch.					☕	☕	☕
Ali **seldom** drinks tea with lunch.						☕	☕
Georgia **rarely** drinks tea with lunch.							☕
Joy never **drinks** tea with lunch.							

■ **EXERCISE 2—ORAL:**   Find the SUBJECTS and VERBS in the sentences. Then add the FREQUENCY ADVERBS in italics to the sentences.

1. *always*   I eat breakfast.   → *I always eat breakfast.*
2. *usually*   I get up at 7:00.
3. *often*   I drink two cups of coffee in the morning.
4. *never*   I eat carrots for breakfast.
5. *seldom*   I watch TV in the morning.
6. *sometimes*   I have tea with dinner.
7. *usually*   Bob eats lunch at the cafeteria.
8. *rarely*   Ann drinks tea.

9. *always*　　　I do my homework.
10. *often*　　　We listen to music after dinner.
11. *never*　　　John and Sue watch TV in the afternoon.
12. *always*　　　The students speak English in the classroom.

■ **EXERCISE 3—ORAL:** Use *always*, *usually*, *often*, *sometimes*, *seldom*, *rarely*, and *never* to talk about your activities (your habits) after 5:00 P.M. every day.

1. eat dinner
2. eat dinner at six o'clock
3. eat dinner at eight o'clock
4. watch TV
5. listen to music
6. go to a movie
7. go shopping
8. go dancing
9. go swimming
10. spend time with my friends
11. talk on the phone
12. speak English
13. write a letter
14. read a newspaper
15. study
16. study English grammar
17. drink milk
18. play with my children
19. kiss my husband/wife
20. have a snack
21. go to bed
22. go to bed at eleven o'clock
23. go to bed after midnight
24. go to bed early
25. go to bed late
26. turn off the lights
27. dream
28. dream in English

2-3 USING FREQUENCY ADVERBS WITH *BE*

SUBJECT + *BE* + FREQUENCY ADVERB	
Tom + *is* + { *always* *usually* *often* *sometimes* *seldom* *rarely* *never* } + late for class.	Frequency adverbs follow *be*.
SUBJECT + FREQUENCY ADVERB + OTHER SIMPLE PRESENT VERBS	
Tom + { *always* *usually* *often* *sometimes* *seldom* *rarely* *never* } + *comes* late.	Frequency adverbs come before all simple present verbs except *be*.

■ **EXERCISE 4:** Add the FREQUENCY ADVERB in *italics* to the sentence.

1. *always*
   always
   Ann is on time for class.

2. *always*
   always
   Ann comes to class on time.

3. *often*   Sue is late for class.

4. *often*   Sue comes to class late.

5. *never*   Ron is happy.

6. *never*   Ron smiles.

7. *usually*   Bob is at home in the evening.

8. *usually*   Bob stays at home in the evening.

9. *seldom*   Tom studies at the library in the evening.

10. *seldom*   Tom is at the library in the evening.

11. *rarely*   I eat breakfast.

12. *often*   I take the bus to school.

13. *usually* The weather is hot in July.

14. *never*   Sue drinks coffee.

15. *sometimes* She drinks tea.

■ **EXERCISE 5—WRITTEN:** Describe a typical day in your life, from the time you get up in the morning until you go to bed. Use the following words to show the order of your activities: ***then, next, at . . . o'clock, after that, later***.

Example: I usually get up at seven-thirty. I shave, brush my teeth, and take a shower. Then I put on my clothes and go to the student cafeteria for breakfast. After that I go back to my room. I sometimes watch the news on TV. At 8:15 I leave the dormitory. I go to class. My class begins at 8:30. I'm in class from 8:30 to 11:30. After that I eat lunch. I usually have a sandwich and a cup of tea for lunch. *(Continue until you complete your day.)*

2-4 PRONUNCIATION OF FINAL -S: /Z/ AND /S/

	VOICED			VOICELESS		
(a)	/b/	rub	(b)	/p/	sleep	Some sounds are "voiced." You use your voice box to make voiced sounds. For example, the sound /b/ comes from your voice box. The final sounds in (a) are voiced.
	/d/	ride		/t/	write	
	/v/	drive		/f/	laugh	
						Some sounds are "voiceless." You don't use your voice box. You push air through your teeth and lips. For example, the sound /p/ comes from air through your lips. The final sounds in (b) are voiceless.
(c)	rubs = *rub*/z/		(d)	sleeps = *sleep*/s/		Final **-s** is pronounced /z/ after voiced sounds, as in (c).
	rides = *ride*/z/			writes = *write*/s/		Final **-s** is pronounced /s/ after voiceless sounds, as in (d).
	drives = *drive*/z/			laughs = *laugh*/s/		

I can feel my voice box. It vibrates.

■ **EXERCISE 6:** The final sounds of the VERBS in these sentences are "voiced." Final **-s** is pronounced /z/. Read the sentences aloud.

1. Cindy rides the bus to school.
   ride/z/

2. Jack usually drives his car to school.
   drive/z/

3. Rain falls.
   fall/z/

4. Sally often dreams about her boyfriend.
   dream/z/

5. Sometimes Jim runs to class.
   run/z/

6. Tina wears blue jeans every day.
   wear/z/

7. Ann always sees Mr. Lee at the market.
   see/z/

Find the VERB in each sentence. Pronounce it. Then read the sentence aloud.

8. The teacher often stands in the front of the room.

9. George lives in the dormitory.

10. Jean rarely smiles.

11. Sam always comes to class on time.

12. It rains a lot in Seattle.

13. Jack always remembers his wife's birthday.

14. It snows in New York City in the winter.

■ **EXERCISE 7:**   The final sounds of the VERBS in these sentences are "voiceless." Final **-s** is
pronounced /s/. Read the sentences aloud.

1. Mike sleeps for eight hours every night.
        sleep/s/
2. Our teacher always helps us.
                      help/s/
3. Jack writes a letter to his girlfriend every day.
        write/s/
4. Sara never laughs.
              laugh/s/
5. Sue usually drinks a cup of coffee in the morning.
                drink/s/
6. Kate walks to school every day.
        walk/s/

Find the VERB in each sentence. Pronounce it. Then read the sentence aloud.

7. My child often claps her hands.

8. Olga always bites her pencil in class.

9. Maria usually gets up at seven-thirty.

10. Yoko asks a lot of questions in class.

11. Ahmed always talks in class.

12. Sue coughs because she smokes.

2-5 SPELLING AND PRONUNCIATION OF FINAL -ES

		SPELLING	PRONUNCIATION	
-sh	(a) push →	*pushes*	*push/əz/*	Ending of verb: **-sh, -ch, -ss, -x.**
-ch	(b) teach →	*teaches*	*teach/əz/*	Spelling: add **-es**.
-ss	(c) kiss →	*kisses*	*kiss/əz/*	Pronunciation: /əz/.
-x	(d) fix →	*fixes*	*fix/əz/*	

■ **EXERCISE 8:** Use the VERBS in *italics* to complete the sentences.

1. *brush*   Anita _____*brushes*_____ her hair every morning.

2. *teach*   Alex _____ English.

3. *fix*   A mechanic _____ cars.

4. *drink*   Sonya _____ tea every afternoon.

5. *watch*   Joon–Kee often _____ television at night.

6. *kiss*   Peter always _____ his children goodnight.

7. *wear*   Tina usually _____ jeans to class.

8. *wash*   Eric seldom _____ dishes.

9. *walk*   Jessica _____ her dog twice each day.

10. *stretch,   When Don gets up in the morning, he _____
    yawn*

    and _____.

2-6 ADDING FINAL -S/-ES TO WORDS THAT END IN -Y

(a) **cry** → **cries** **try** → **tries**	End of verb: consonant + **-y**. Spelling: change **y** to **i**, add **-es**.
(b) **pay** → **pays** **enjoy** → **enjoys**	End of verb: vowel + **-y**. Spelling: add **-s**.

■ **EXERCISE 9:** Use the words in *italics* to complete the sentences.

1. *pay, always*   Boris _____*always pays*_____ his bills on time.

2. *cry, seldom*   Our baby _____ at night.

3. *study*   Paul _____ at the library every day.

4. *stay, usually*   Jean _____ home at night.

5. *fly*   Kunio is a pilot. He _____ a plane.

6. *carry, always*   Carol _____ her books to class.

7. *pray*   Jack _____ every day.

8. *buy, seldom*   Ann _____ new clothes.

9. *worry*   Tina is a good student, but she _____
                     about her grades.

10. *enjoy*   Don _____ good food.

2-7 IRREGULAR SINGULAR VERBS: *HAS, DOES, GOES*

(a) I *have* a book. (b) He *has* a book.	she he it }	+ *has* /hæz/	**Have, do,** and *go* have irregular forms for third person singular: have → has do → does go → goes
(c) I *do* my work. (d) She *does* her work.	she he it }	+ *does* /dəz/	
(e) They *go* to school. (f) She *goes* to school.	she he it }	+ *goes* /gowz/	

■ **EXERCISE 10:**   Use the given VERBS to complete the sentences.

1. *do*   Pierre always _____*does*_____ his homework.

2. *do*   We always _____*do*_____ our homework.

3. *have*   Yoko and Kunio _____ their books.

4. *have*   Ali _____ a car.

5. *go*   Bill _____ to school every day.

6. *go*   My friends often _____ to the beach.

7. *do*   Anna seldom _____ her homework.

8. *do*   We _____ exercises in class every day.

9. *go, go*   Roberto _____ downtown every weekend. He and his wife

_____ shopping.

10. *have*   Jessica _____ a snack every night around ten.

	SPELLING	PRONUNCIATION	
(a)	rub → *rubs* ride → *rides* smile → *smiles* dream → *dreams* run → *runs* wear → *wears* drive → *drives* see → *sees* snow → *snows*	*rub*/z/ *ride*/z/ *smile*/z/ *dream*/z/ *run*/z/ *wear*/z/ *drive*/z/ *see*/z/ *snow*/z/	To form a simple present verb in 3rd person singular, you usually add only **-s**, as in (a) and (b). In (a): **-s** is pronounced /z/. The final sounds in (a) are *voiced*.
(b)	drink → *drinks* sleep → *sleeps* write → *writes* laugh → *laughs*	*drink*/s/ *sleep*/s/ *write*/s/ *laugh*/s/	In (b): **-s** is pronounced /s/. The final sounds in (b) are *voiceless*.
(c)	push → *pushes* teach → *teaches* kiss → *kisses* fix → *fixes*	*push*/əz/ *teach*/əz/ *kiss*/əz/ *fix*/əz/	End of verb: **-sh, -ch, -ss, -x** Spelling: add **-es** Pronunciation: /əz/
(d)	cry → *cries* study → *studies*	*cry*/z/ *study*/z/	End of verb: consonant + **-y** Spelling: change **y** to **i**, add **-es**
(e)	pay → *pays* buy → *buys*	*pay*/z/ *buy*/z/	End of verb: vowel + **-y** Spelling: add **-s**
(f)	have → **has** go → **goes** do → **does**	/hæz/ /gowz/ /dəz/	The 3rd person singular forms of *have, go,* and *do* are irregular.

■ **EXERCISE 11—ORAL (BOOKS CLOSED):** Talk about everyday activities using the given

    VERB.

Example:
TEACHER: eat
STUDENT A: I eat breakfast every morning.
TEACHER: What does (. . .) do every morning?
STUDENT B: He/She eats breakfast.

TEACHER: eat
STUDENT A: I always eat dinner at the student cafeteria.
TEACHER: What does (. . .) always do?
STUDENT B: He/She always eats dinner at the student cafeteria.

1. eat	6. study	11. listen to
2. go	7. get up	12. wash
3. drink	8. watch	13. put on
4. brush	9. speak	14. carry
5. have	10. do	15. kiss

■ **EXERCISE 12—ORAL (BOOKS CLOSED):**   Tell a classmate about your usual habits in the morning. (Look at the list you made for Exercise 1 if you wish.) Your classmate will then write a summary of your daily morning habits.

Directions:

STUDENT A: *Tell Student B ten to fifteen things you do every morning.*
STUDENT B: *Take notes while Student A is talking. (You will use these notes later to write a paragraph about Student A's usual morning habits.)*

Then switch roles.

STUDENT B: *Tell Student A ten to fifteen things you do every morning.*
STUDENT A: *Take notes while Student B is talking.*

When you finish talking, each of you should write a paragraph about the other person's daily morning activities. Pay special attention to final **-s/-es.**

■ **EXERCISE 13:**   Complete the sentences. Use the words in parentheses. Use the SIMPLE PRESENT TENSE. Pay special attention to singular and plural, to spelling, and to pronunciation of final **-s/-es.**

1. The students *(ask, often)* _____*often ask*_____ questions in class.

2. Pablo *(study, usually)* _____ at the library every evening.

3. Olga *(bite)* _____ her fingernails when she is nervous.

4. Don *(cash)* _____ a check at the bank once a week.

5. Sometimes I *(worry)* _____ about my grades at school.

   Sonya *(worry, never)* _____ about her grades.

   She *(study)* _____ hard.

6. Ms. Jones and Mr. Anderson *(teach)* _____ at the local high school. Ms. Jones *(teach)* _____ math.

7. Birds *(fly)* _____. They *(have)* _____ wings.

8. A bird *(fly)* _____. It *(have)* _____ wings.

9. Jason *(do, always)* _____ his homework. He

   (go, never) _____ to bed until his homework is finished.

10. Mr. Cook *(say, always)** _____ hello to his neighbor in the morning.

11. Ms. Chu *(pay, always)** _____ attention in class. She *(answer)* _____ questions. She *(listen)* _____ to the teacher. She *(ask)* _____ questions.

12. Sam *(enjoy)* _____ cooking. He *(try, often)* _____ to make new recipes. He *(like)* _____ to have company for dinner. He *(invite)* _____ me to dinner once a month. When I arrive, I *(go)* _____ to the kitchen and *(watch)* _____ him cook. He *(have, usually)* _____ three or four pots on the stove. He *(watch)* _____ the pots carefully. He *(make)* _____ a big mess in the kitchen when he cooks. After dinner, he *(wash, always)* _____ all the dishes and *(clean)* _____ the kitchen. I *(cook, never)* _____. It *(be)* _____ too much trouble. But my friend Sam *(love)* _____ to cook.

*Pronunciation of **says** = /sɛz/. Pronunciation of **pays** = /peyz/.

2-9 THE SIMPLE PRESENT: NEGATIVE

(a) **I** *do not* drink coffee. **We** *do not* drink coffee. **You** *do not* drink coffee. **They** *do not* drink coffee. (b) **She** *does not* drink coffee. **He** *does not* drink coffee. **It** *does not* drink coffee.	NEGATIVE: *I* *we* *you* *they* } + *do not* + main verb
	she *he* *it* } + *does not* + main verb
	Do and *does* are called "helping verbs."
	Notice in (b): In 3rd person singular, there is no *-s* on the main verb; the final *-s* is part of *does*. INCORRECT: *She does not drinks coffee.*
(c) I *don't* drink tea. They *don't* have a car. (d) He *doesn't* drink tea. Mary *doesn't* have a car.	CONTRACTIONS: *do not* = *don't* *does not* = *doesn't* People usually use contractions when they speak. People often use contractions when they write.

■ **EXERCISE 14:** Use the words in *italics* to make NEGATIVE SENTENCES.

1. *like, not* Ingrid _____*doesn't like*_____ tea.

2. *like, not* I _____*don't like*_____ tea.

3. *know, not* Mary and Jim are strangers. Mary _____ Jim.

4. *need, not* It's a nice day today. You _____ your umbrella.

5. *snow, not* It _____ in Bangkok in the winter.

6. *speak, not* I _____ French.

7. *be, not* I _____ hungry.

8. *live, not* Butterflies _____ long.

9. *have, not* A butterfly _____ a long life.

10. *be, not* A butterfly _____ large.

11. *be, not* Butterflies _____ large.

12. *have, not* We _____ class every day.

13. *have, not*   This city _____ nice weather in the summer.

14. *be, not*   It _____ cold today.

15. *rain, not*   It _____ every day.

■ **EXERCISE 15:**   Complete the sentences. Use the words in parentheses. Use the SIMPLE PRESENT TENSE.

1. Alex *(like)* _____*likes*_____ tea, but he *(like, not)* _____*doesn't like*_____ coffee.

2. Sara *(know)* _____ Ali, but she *(know, not)* _____

   _____ Hiroshi.

3. Pablo and Maria *(want)* _____ to stay home tonight. They *(want, not)*

   _____ to go to a movie.

4. Robert *(be, not)* _____ hungry. He *(want, not)* _____

   _____ a sandwich.

5. Mr. Smith *(drink, not)* _____ coffee, but Mr. Jones

   (drink) _____ twelve cups every day.

6. I *(be, not)* _____ rich. I *(have, not)* _____
   a lot of money.

7. This pen *(belong, not)* _____ to me. It *(belong)*

   _____ to Pierre.

8. My friends *(live, not)* _____ in the dorm. They *(have)*

   _____ an apartment.

9. It *(be)* _____ a nice day today. It *(be, not)* _____ cold. You

   (need, not) _____ your coat.

10. Today *(be)* _____ a holiday. We *(have, not)* _____
    class today.

■ **EXERCISE 16:** Use verbs from the list to complete the sentences. Make all of the sentences NEGATIVE by using **does + not** or **do + not**.

carry	*go*	*smoke*
do	*shave*	*speak*
drink	*make*	
eat	*put on*	

1. Bob _____*doesn't go*_____ to school every day.

2. My roommates are from Japan. They _____ Spanish.

3. Fred has a beard. He _____ in the morning.

4. Sue has a briefcase. She _____ a bookbag to class.

5. We _____ to class on Sunday.

6. Sally takes care of her health. She _____ cigarettes.

7. Jane and Alex always have lunch at home. They _____ at the cafeteria.

8. Sometimes I _____ my homework in the evening. I watch TV instead.

9. Jack is a careful writer. He _____ mistakes in spelling when he writes.

10. My sister likes tea, but she _____ coffee.

11. I'm lazy. I _____ exercises in the morning.

12. Sometimes Ann _____ her shoes when she goes outside. She likes to walk barefoot in the grass.

■ EXERCISE 17—ORAL (BOOKS CLOSED): Use *not*.

TEACHER: eat breakfast every day
STUDENT A: I don't eat breakfast every day.
TEACHER: Tell me about (Student A).
STUDENT B: She/He doesn't eat breakfast every day.

1. walk to school every day
2. shave every day
3. read a newspaper every day
4. go shopping every day
5. study grammar every day
6. watch TV every day

7. write a letter every day
8. go dancing every day
9. drink coffee every day
10. eat lunch every day
11. listen to music every day
12. come to class every day

■ EXERCISE 18—ORAL: Use the given words to make truthful sentences.

1. Grass \ be blue. → *Grass isn't blue.*
2. Grass \ be green. → *Grass is green.*
3. Dogs \ have tails. → *Dogs have tails.*
4. People* \ have tails. → *People don't have tails.*
5. A restaurant \ sell shoes.
6. A restaurant \ serve food.
7. People \ wear clothes.
8. Animals \ wear clothes.
9. A child \ need love, food, care, and toys.
10. A child \ need a driver's license.
11. Refrigerators \ be hot inside.
12. Refrigerators \ be cold inside.
13. Electricity \ be visible.
14. Light \ be visible.
15. Fresh vegetables \ be good for you.
16. Junk food** \ be good for you.
17. Cats \ have whiskers.
18. Birds \ have whiskers.

19. An architect \ design buildings.
20. Doctors \ design buildings.
21. Doctors \ take care of sick people.
22. A bus \ carry people from one place to another.
23. The weather \ be very hot today.
24. It \ be very cold today.
25. Glass \ break.
26. Rubber \ be flexible.
27. Rubber \ break.
28. English \ be an easy language to learn.
29. People in this city \ be friendly.
30. It \ rain a lot in this city.
31. Apples \ have seeds.
32. Scientists \ have all the answers to the mysteries of the universe.

---

*People is a plural noun. It takes a plural verb.
**Junk food is food that has a lot of fat and/or sugar, but little nutritional value.

2-10 THE SIMPLE PRESENT: YES/NO QUESTIONS

DO/DOES + SUBJECT + MAIN VERB			QUESTION FORMS, SIMPLE PRESENT

DO/DOES + SUBJECT + MAIN VERB	QUESTION FORMS, SIMPLE PRESENT
(a) **Do** *you* *like* coffee? (b) **Does** **Bob** *like* coffee?	**Do I** **Do you** **Do we** } + *main verb (simple form)* **Do they** **Does she** **Does he** } + *main verb (simple form)* **Does it**
	Notice in (b): The main verb in the question does not have a final *-s*. The final *-s* is part of **does.** INCORRECT: *Does Bob like**s** coffee?*
(c) **Are you** a student? (d) INCORRECT: *Do you be a student?*	When the main verb is a form of **be, do** is NOT used. See Chart 1-9 for question forms with **be.**

QUESTION	SHORT ANSWER + (LONG ANSWER)	
(e) *Do* you *like* tea? →	Yes, I **do**. (I *like* tea.) No, I **don't**. (I *don't like* tea.)	**Do, don't, does,** and **doesn't** are used in the short answers to yes/ no questions in the simple present.
(f) *Does* Bob *like* tea? →	Yes, he **does**. (He *likes* tea.) No, he **doesn't**. (He *doesn't like* tea.)	

■ **EXERCISE 19:** Make questions. Give short answers.

1. A: ___*Do you like tea?*___

   B: ___*Yes, I do.*___ (I like tea.)

2. A: ___*Do you like coffee?*___

   B: ___*No, I don't.*___ (I don't like coffee.)

3. A: _____

   B: _____ (I don't speak Japanese.)

4. A: _____

   B: _____ (Ann speaks French.)

5. A: _____

   B: _____ (Ann and Tom don't speak Arabic.)

6. A: _____

    B: _____ (I do exercises every morning.)

7. A: _____

    B: _____ (I don't have a Spanish-English dictionary.)

8. A: _____

    B: _____ (Sue has a cold.)

9. A: _____

    B: _____ (The teacher comes to class every day.)

10. A: _____

    B: _____ (Jim and Sue don't do their homework every day.)

11. A: _____

    B: _____ (It rains a lot in April.)

12. A: _____

    B: _____ (My parents live in Baghdad.)

■ **EXERCISE 20—ORAL (BOOKS CLOSED):** Ask and answer questions.

TEACHER: walk to school every day
STUDENT A: Do you walk to school every day?
STUDENT B: Yes, I do.   OR: No, I don't.
STUDENT A: Does *(Student B)* walk to school every day?
STUDENT C: Yes, he/she does.   OR: No, he/she doesn't.

1. walk to school every day
2. watch TV every day
3. eat breakfast every day
4. speak English every day
5. come to class every day
6. get up at seven o'clock every day
7. talk on the phone every day
8. go to the bank every day

9. wear blue jeans every day
10. have a car
11. have a bicycle
12. like ice cream
13. like *(name of city)*
14. live in *(name of a hotel)*
15. live in an apartment
16. go shopping every day

■ **EXERCISE 21:** Make questions. Give short answers. Use the names of your classmates in the questions.

1. A: ___*Does (Carlos) speak English?*_____

    B: ___*Yes, he does.*_____ (He speaks English.)

2. A: _Does (Yoko) speak Spanish?_ _____

   B: _No, she doesn't._ _____ (She doesn't speak Spanish.)

3. A: _Is (Ali) in class today?_ _____

   B: _No, he isn't._ _____ (He isn't in class today.)

4. A: _____

   B: _____ (He comes to class every day.)

5. A: _____

   B: _____ (They're in class today.)

6. A: _____

   B: _____ (She sits in the same seat every day.)

7. A: _____

   B: _____ (He has a mustache.)

8. A: _____

   B: _____ (She doesn't have a bicycle.)

9. A: _____

   B: _____ (He's wearing blue jeans today.)

10. A: _____

    B: _____ (He wears blue jeans every day.)

11. A: _____

    B: _____ (They aren't from Indonesia.)

12: A: _____

    B: _____ (They don't have dictionaries on their desks.)

13. A: _____

    B: _____ (She's writing in her book right now.)

14. A: _____

    B: _____ (She studies hard.)

15. A: _____

    B: _____ (They speak English.)

2-11 THE SIMPLE PRESENT: ASKING INFORMATION QUESTIONS WITH *WHERE*

(WHERE) +	*DO/DOES* +	SUBJECT +	MAIN VERB		SHORT ANSWER
(a)	*Do*	they	*live*	in Tokyo? →	*Yes*, they do. / *No*, they don't.
(b) *Where*	*do*	they	*live?*	→	*In Tokyo.*
(c)	*Does*	Gina	*live*	in Rome? →	*Yes*, she does. / *No*, she doesn't.
(d) *Where*	*does*	Gina	*live?*	→	*In Rome*.

NOTE: (a) and (c) are called "yes/no questions." The answer to these questions can be *yes* or *no*. (b) and (d) are called "information questions." The answer gives information. *Where* asks for information about place.

Notice in the examples: The form of yes/no questions and information questions is the same:
DO/DOES + SUBJECT + MAIN VERB

■ **EXERCISE 22:** Make questions.

1. A: ___*Does Jean eat lunch at the cafeteria every day?*___
   B: Yes, she does. (Jean eats lunch at the cafeteria every day.)

2. A: ___*Where does Jean eat lunch every day?*___
   B: At the cafeteria. (Jean eats lunch at the cafeteria every day.)

3. A: _____
   B: At the post office. (Peter works at the post office.)

4. A: _____
   B: Yes, he does. (Peter works at the post office.)

5. A: _____
   B: Yes, I do. (I live in an apartment.)

6. A: _____
   B: In an apartment. (I live in an apartment.)

7. A: _____
   B: At a restaurant. (Bill eats dinner at a restaurant every day.)

8. A: _____
   B: In the front row. (I sit in the front row during class.)

9. A: _____
   B: At the University of Wisconsin. (Jessica goes to school at the University of Wisconsin.)

10. A: _____
    B: On my desk. (My book is on my desk.)

11. A: _____
    B: To class. (I go to class every morning.)

12. A: _____
    B: In class. (The students are in class right now.)

13. A: _____
    B: In Australia. (Kangaroos live in Australia.)

■ **EXERCISE 23:—ORAL (BOOKS CLOSED):**   Ask a classmate a question. Use ***where.***

Example: live
STUDENT A: Where do you live?
STUDENT B: *(free response)*

1. live
2. eat lunch every day
3. sit during class
4. study at night
5. go to school
6. buy school supplies
7. buy your groceries
8. go on weekends

9. go after class
10. eat dinner
11. be *(name of a student in this room)*
12. be *(names of two students)*
13. be *(name of a country or city)*
14. be *(names of two countries or cities)*
15. be *(something a student owns)*
16. be *(some things a student owns)*

2-12 THE SIMPLE PRESENT: ASKING INFORMATION QUESTIONS WITH *WHEN* AND *WHAT TIME*

Q-WORD* + *DOES/DO* + SUBJECT + MAIN VERB	SHORT ANSWER
(a) **When** do you go to class? →	*At nine o'clock.*
(b) **What time** do you go to class? →	*At nine o'clock.*
(c) **When** does Anna eat dinner? →	*At six P.M.*
(d) **What time** does Anna eat dinner? →	*At six P.M.*
(e) What time *do you **usually*** go to class?	The frequency adverb ***usually*** comes immediately after the subject in a question. QUESTION WORD + ***DOES/DO*** + SUBJECT + ***USUALLY*** + MAIN VERB

*A "Q-word" is a "question word." *Where, when, what, what time, who,* and *why* are examples of question words.

■ **EXERCISE 24:** Make questions.

1. A: ___*When/What time do you eat breakfast?*___
   B: At 7:30 (I eat breakfast at 7:30 in the morning.)

2. A: ___*When/What time do you usually eat breakfast?*___
   B: At 7:00. (Alex usually eats breakfast at 7:00.)

   3. A: _____
      B: At 6:45. (I get up at 6:45.)

4. A: _____
   B: At 6:30. (Maria usually gets up at 6:30.)

   5. A: _____
      B: At 8:15. (The movie starts at 8:15.)

6. A: _____
   B: Around 11:00. (I usually go to bed around 11:00.)

   7. A: _____
      B: At half-past twelve. (I usually eat lunch at half-past twelve.)

8. A: _____
   B: At 5:30. (The restaurant opens at 5:30.)

   9. A: _____
      B: At 9:05. (The train leaves at 9:05.)

10. A: _____
    B: Between 6:30 and 8:00. (I usually eat dinner between 6:30 and 8:00.)

11. A: _____

    B: At 10:00 P.M. (The library closes at 10:00 P.M. on Saturday.)

12. A: _____

    B: At a quarter past eight. (My classes begin at a quarter past eight.)

■ **EXERCISE 25—ORAL (BOOKS CLOSED):** Ask a classmate a question. Use **when** or **what time**.

Example: eat breakfast
STUDENT A: When/What time do you eat breakfast?
STUDENT B: *(free response)*

1. get up
2. usually get up
3. eat breakfast
4. leave home in the morning
5. usually get to class
6. eat lunch
7. go back home
8. get home
9. have dinner
10. usually study in the evening
11. go to bed

2-13	SUMMARY: INFORMATION QUESTIONS WITH *BE* AND *DO*

	Q-WORD	+	*BE*	+	SUBJECT		LONG ANSWER
(a)	Where		*is*		Thailand?	→	Thailand *is* in Southeast Asia.
(b)	Where		*are*		your books?	→	My books *are* on my desk.
(c)	When		*is*		the concert?	→	The concert *is* on April 3rd.
(d)	What		*is*		your name?	→	My name *is* Yoko.
(e)	What time		*is*		it?	→	It *is* ten-thirty.

	Q-WORD	+	*DO*	+	SUBJECT	+	MAIN VERB		LONG ANSWER
(f)	Where		*do*		you		*live?*	→	I *live* in Los Angeles.
(g)	What time		*does*		the plane		*arrive?*	→	The plane *arrives* at six-fifteen.
(h)	What		*do*		monkeys		*eat?*	→	Monkeys *eat* fruit, plants, and insects.
(k)	When		*does*		Bob		*study?*	→	Bob *studies* in the evenings.

NOTICE: In questions with *be* as the main and only verb, the subject follows *be*. In simple present questions with verbs other than *be*, the subject comes between *do/does* and the main verb.

■ **EXERCISE 26:** Complete the questions in the dialogues by using *is, are, does,* or *do.*

DIALOGUE ONE

(1) A: What time _____ the movie start?

(2) B: Seven-fifteen. _____ you want to go with us?

(3) A: Yes. What time _____ it now?

(4) B: Almost seven o'clock. _____ you ready to leave?
    A: Yes, let's go.

DIALOGUE TWO

(5) A: Where _____ my keys to the car?

(6) B: I don't know. Where _____ you usually keep them?
    A: In my purse. But they're not there.
    B: Are you sure?

(7) A: Yes. _____ you see them?

(8) B: No. _____ they in one of your pockets?
    A: I don't think so.

(9) B: _____ your husband have them?
    A: No. He has his own set of car keys.
    B: Well, I hope you find them.
    A: Thanks.

DIALOGUE THREE

(10) A: _____ you go to school?
     B: Yes.

(11) A: _____ your brother go to school too?
     B: No. He quit school last semester. He has a job now.

(12) A: _____ it a good job?

B: Not really.

(13) A: Where _____ he work?

B: At a restaurant. He washes dishes.

(14) A: _____ he live with you?

B: No, he lives with my parents.

(15) A: _____ your parents unhappy that he quit school?

B: They're very unhappy about it.

(16) A: _____ they want him to return to school?

B: Of course. They don't want him to be a dishwasher for the rest of his life. They have many dreams for him and his future.

■ **EXERCISE 27:** Complete the dialogues with appropriate questions.

1. A: ___*What time does the concert begin?*___
   B: At eight. (The concert begins at eight.)

2. A: ___*Is San Francisco foggy in the winter?*___
   B: Yes, it is. (San Francisco is foggy in the winter.)

3. A: _____
   B: In May. (The weather starts to get hot in May.)

4. A: _____
   B: Yes. (I dream in color.)

5. A: _____
   B: Yes. (Igor comes from Russia.)

6. A: _____
   B: Russia. (Olga comes from Russia.)

7. A: _____
   B: Yes, he is. (Ivan is from Russia.)

8. A: _____
   B: In Moscow. (Red Square is in Moscow.)

9. A: _____
   B: Yes. (Birds sleep.)

   A: _____
   B: In trees and bushes or in their nests. (They sleep in trees and bushes or in their nests.)

Blue whale

10. A: _____
    B: The blue whale. (The biggest animal on earth is the blue whale.)

11. A: _____
    B: No, they aren't. (Whales aren't fish.)

    A: _____
    B: Yes, they are. (They are mammals.)

    A: _____
    B: Yes, they do. (They breathe air.)

12. A: _____
    B: No, it isn't. (A seahorse isn't a mammal.)

13. A: _____
    B: A very small fish that looks a little like a horse.
       (A seahorse is a very small fish that looks
       a little like a horse.)

Seahorse

14. A: _____
    B: Yes. (A starfish has a mouth.)

    A: _____
    B: In the middle of its underside. (It is in the middle of its underside.)

    A: _____
    B: Clams, oysters, and shrimp. (A starfish eats clams, oysters, and shrimp.)

Starfish

■ **EXERCISE 28:** Complete the dialogues with your own words.

1. A: Do _____?
   B: No, I don't.

2. A: Where are _____?
   B: I don't know.

3. A: What time does _____?

   B: _____

4. A: When do _____?

   B: _____

5. A: Is _____?

   B: _____

6. A: What is _____?

   B: _____

7. A: Are _____?

   B: _____

8. A: What are _____?

   B: _____

9. A: What do _____?

   B: _____

10. A: What does _____?

   B: _____

■ **EXERCISE 29—ORAL/WRITTEN:** Interview someone (a friend, a roommate, a classmate, etc.) about her/his daily schedule. Use the information from the interview to write a composition.

Some questions you might want to ask during the interview:

What do you do every morning?
What do you do every afternoon?
What do you do every evening?

What time do you . . . ?
When do you . . . ?
Where do you . . . ?

2-14 USING *IT* TO TALK ABOUT TIME

QUESTION	ANSWER	
(a) What day is it?	*It's* Monday.	In English, people use *it* to express (to talk about) time.
(b) What month is it?	*It's* September.	
(c) What year is it?	*It's* _____.	Look at Appendixes 2 and 3 in the back of the book for lists of days, months, and numbers.
(d) What's the date today?	*It's* September 15th.	
	It's the 15th of September.	
(e) What time is it?	*It's* 9:00.★	Look at Appendix 4 in the back of the book for ways of saying the time.
	It's nine.	
	It's nine o'clock.	
	It's nine (o'clock) A.M.	

★American English uses a colon (two dots) between the hour and the minutes: 9:00 A.M. British English uses one dot: 9.00 A.M.

■ **EXERCISE 30:** Make questions. Use *what* in your questions.

1. A: _____*What day is it?*_____
   B: It's Tuesday.

2. A: _____
   B: It's March 14th.

3. A: _____
   B: Ten-thirty.

4. A: _____
   B: March.

5. A: _____
   B: It's six-fifteen.

6. A: _____
   B: The 1st of April.

7. A: _____
   B: Wednesday.

8. A: _____
   B: July 3rd.

9. A: _____
   B: It's 6:05.

10. A: _____
    B: It's 10:55.

2-15 PREPOSITIONS OF TIME

at	(a) We have class **at** one o'clock. (b) I have an appointment with the doctor **at** 3:00. (c) We sleep **at** night.	**at** + a specific time on the clock **at** + *night*
in	(d) My birthday is **in** October. (e) I was born **in** 1960. (f) We have class **in** the morning. (g) Bob has class **in** the afternoon. (h) I study **in** the evening.	**in** + specific month **in** + specific year **in** + *the morning* **in** + *the afternoon* **in** + *the evening*
on	(i) I have class **on** Monday. (j) I was born **on** October 31, 1975.	**on** + a specific day of the week **on** + a specific date
from ... to	(k) We have class **from** 1:00 **to** 2:00.	**from** (a specific time) **to** (a specific time)

■ **EXERCISE 31:** Complete the sentences with PREPOSITIONS OF TIME.

1. We have class _____*at*_____ ten o'clock.

2. We have class _____ ten _____ eleven.

3. I have class _____ the morning.

4. I work _____ the afternoon.

5. I study _____ the evening.

6. I sleep _____ night.

7. I was born _____ May.

8. I was born _____ 1979.

9. I was born _____ May 25.

10. I was born _____ May 25, 1979.

11. The post office isn't open _____ Sunday.

12. The post office is open _____ 8:00 A.M. _____ 5:00 P.M. Monday.

13. The post office closes _____ 5:00 P.M.

1. Jane has an appointment with the dentist _____ ten-thirty.

2. We go to class _____ the morning.

3. The bank is open _____ Friday, but it isn't open _____ Saturday.

4. My birthday is _____ February.

5. I was born _____ February 14, 1973.

6. I watch television _____ the evening.

7. I go to bed _____ night.

8. The bank is open _____ 9:00 A.M. _____ 4:00 P.M.

9. I was in high school _____ 1988.

10. Our classes begin _____ January 10.

11. I study at the library _____ the afternoon.

12. We have a vacation _____ August.

2-16 USING *IT* TO TALK ABOUT THE WEATHER

(a) **It's** sunny today. (b) **It's** hot and humid today. (c) **It's** a nice day today.	In English, people usually use *it* when they talk about the weather.
(d) **What's the weather like** in Istanbul in January? (e) **How's the weather** in Moscow in the summer?	People commonly ask about the weather by saying: *What's the weather like?* OR: *How's the weather?*

■ **EXERCISE 33—ORAL:** How's the weather today? Use these words to talk about today's weather.

Example: hot
Response: It's hot today. OR: It isn't / It's not hot today.

1. hot	7. cloudy	13. gloomy
2. warm	8. partly cloudy	14. humid
3. cool	9. clear	15. muggy
4. chilly	10. nice	16. stormy
5. cold	11. windy	17. freezing
6. sunny	12. foggy	18. below freezing

■ **EXERCISE 34—ORAL:** Change the Fahrenheit temperatures to Celsius by choosing temperatures from the list. Then describe the temperature in words.

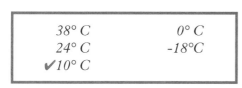

38° C	0° C
24° C	-18°C
✔10° C	

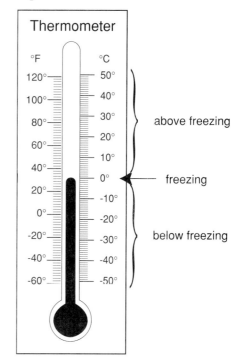

FARENHEIT	CELSIUS	DESCRIPTION
1. 50°F	_10°C_	_cool, chilly_
2. 32°F	_____	_____
3. 100°F	_____	_____
4. 75°F	_____	_____
5. 0°F	_____	_____

■ **EXERCISE 35:** "Approximate" means "close but not exact." Here is a fast way to get an **approximate** number when you convert from one temperature system to another.★

> • To change **Celsius to Fahrenheit**: DOUBLE THE CELSIUS NUMBER AND ADD 30.
>
> *Examples:* 12°C x 2 = 24 + 30 = 54°F. (Exact numbers: 12°C = 53.6°F.)
> 20°C x 2 = 40 + 30 = 70°F. (Exact numbers: 20°C = 68°F.)
> 35°C x 2 = 70 + 30 = 100°F. (Exact numbers: 35°C = 95°F.)
>
> • To change **Fahrenheit to Celsius**: SUBTRACT 30 FROM THE FAHRENHEIT NUMBER AND THEN DIVIDE BY 2.
>
> *Examples:* 60°F - 30 = 30 ÷ 2 = 15°C. (Exact numbers: 60°F = 15.6°C.)
> 80°F - 30 = 50 ÷ 2 = 25°C. (Exact numbers: 80°F = 26.7°C.)
> 90°F - 30 = 60 ÷ 2 = 30°C. (Exact numbers: 90°F = 32.2°C.)

Change the following from Celsius to Fahrenheit and Fahrenheit to Celsius. Calculate the **approximate** numbers.

1. 22°C → *22°C = approximately 74°F (22°C x 2 = 44 + 30 = 74°F)*
2. 2°C
3. 30°C
4. 10°C
5. 16°C

6. 45°F
7. 70°F
8. 58°F
9. 100°F

★To get exact numbers, use these formulas: $C = 5/9$ $(°F -32)$ OR $F = 9/5$ $(°C) + 32$.

■ **EXERCISE 36—REVIEW:** Add *-s* or *-es* where necessary. Discuss the correct pronunciation: /s/, /z/, or /əz/.

ABDUL AND PABLO

S (lives = live + /z/)
(1) My friend Abdul live▲ in an apartment near school.   (2) He walk to school almost every day.   (3) Sometimes he catch a bus, especially if it's cold and rainy outside.   (4) Abdul share the apartment with Pablo.   (5) Pablo come from Venezuela. (6) Abdul and Pablo go to the same school.   (7) They take English classes.   (8) Abdul speak Arabic as his first language, and Pablo speak Spanish.   (9) They communicate in English.   (10) Sometimes Abdul try to teach Pablo to speak a little Arabic, and Pablo give Abdul Spanish lessons.   (11) They laugh a lot during the Arabic and Spanish lessons.   (12) Abdul enjoy having Pablo as his roommate, but he miss his family back in Saudi Arabia.

SNAKES

(13) Snakes eat all sorts of things.   (14) Eggs are a favorite food of many snakes. (15) When a snake eat an egg, the snake first curl around the egg. (16) It don't want the egg to roll away.   (17) Then the snake open its mouth and move the egg into its throat. (18) It squeeze the egg with muscles in its neck.   (19) The egg break and go into the snake's stomach.   (20) Then the snake spit out the eggshell. (21) Snakes love to eat eggs.

■ **EXERCISE 37—REVIEW:** Complete the sentences with the words in parentheses. Use the SIMPLE PRESENT of the verbs.

1. *(Anita, go)* _____*Does Anita go*_____ to her uncle's house every day?

2. *(monkeys, eat)* _____ insects?

3. A: I usually *(remember, not)* _____ my dreams.

   (you, remember) _____ your dreams?

B: Sometimes. I often *(write)* _____ my dreams down as soon as

I wake up. I *(like)* _____ to think about my dreams. I *(try)*

_____ to understand them.

4. I *(understand, not)* _____ my brother. He

(have, not) _____ a job or a place to live. He *(sleep)*

_____ at his friends' apartments. He *(take, not)* _____

_____ care of himself. I *(worry)* _____ about him all the time.

5. Ocean waves *(be)* _____ interesting. In an ocean wave, water *(move)*

_____ up and down, but the water *(move, not)* _____

_____ forward. This movement *(be)* _____ the same

as the movement you can see in a rope. If you shake one end of a rope, waves *(run)*

_____ along the rope, but the rope *(move, not)* _____

_____ forward. The water in an ocean wave *(move)* _____

forward only when a wave *(reach)* _____ land. Then an ocean wave *(carry)*

_____ sand and other things forward

when it *(hit)* _____ a sandy beach.

6. A: *(you, study)* _____ a lot?

B: I *(study)* _____ at least three hours every night. My roommate

(study) _____ at least five hours. She's very serious about

her education. How about you? *(you, spend)* _____
a lot of time studying?

A: No, I don't. I *(spend)* _____ as little time as possible. I

(like, not) _____ to study.

B: Then why *(you, be)* _____ a student?

A: My parents *(want)* _____ me to go to school. I *(want, not)*

_____ to be here.

B: In that case, I *(think)* _____ that you should drop out of school

and find a job until you figure out what you want to do with your life.

7. I *(have)* _____ two roommates. One of them, Sam, is always neat

and clean. He *(wash)* _____ his clothes once a week. *(you, know)*

_____ Matt, my other roommate? He *(be)* _____

the opposite of Sam. For example, Matt *(change, not)* _____ the

sheets on his bed. He *(keep)* _____ the same sheets week after

week. He *(wash, never)* _____ his clothes.

He *(wear)* _____ the same dirty jeans every day. Sam's side of the

room *(be, always)* _____ neat, and Matt's side

(be, always) _____ a mess. As my mother always

(say) _____ , it *(take)* _____ all kinds of people

to make a world.

■ **EXERCISE 38—REVIEW:** Complete the dialogues with your own words by asking questions.

1. A: _____
   B: No, I don't.

2. A: _____
   B: Yes, I am.

3. A: _____
   B: In an apartment.

4. A: _____
   B: Six-thirty.

5. A: _____
   B: Monday.

6. A: _____
   B: At home.

7. A: _____
   B: No, he doesn't.

8. A: _____
   B: No, she isn't.

9. A: _____
   B: South of the United States.

10. A: _____
    B: Yes, it is.

11. A: _____
    B: Yes, they do.

12. A: _____
    B: In Southeast Asia.

13. A: _____
    B: Hot in the summer.

14. A: _____
    B: September.

15. A: _____
    B: Yes, I do.

■ **EXERCISE 39—REVIEW:**   Correct the mistakes in the following sentences.

                      lives

1. Yoko ~~live~~ in Japan.

2. Ann comes usually to class on time.

3. Peter watch TV every evening.

4. Anita carry a briefcase to work every day.

5. She enjoy her job.

6. I no know Joe.

7. Mike don't like milk. He never drink it.

8. Tina doesn't speaks Chinese. She speakes Spanish.

9. Do you are a student?

10. Does your roommate sleeps with the window open?

11. A: Do you like strong coffee?

    B: Yes, I like.

12. Where your parents live?

13. What time is your English class begins?

14. Olga isn't need a car. She have a bicycle.

15. Do Pablo does his homework every day?

■ **EXERCISE 40—REVIEW:**   Choose the correct completion.

1. Alex _____ know French.
    A. isn't   B. doesn't   C. don't

2. _____ Alex speak Russian?
    A. Is   B. Does   C. Do

3. _____ Alex from Canada?
    A. Is   B. Does   C. Do

4. When _____ you usually study?
    A. are   B. does   C. do

5. Anita _____ a job.
   A. no have   B. no has   C. doesn't have

6. Omar _____ his new car every Saturday.
   A. wash   B. washs   C. washes

7. Where does Tina _____ to school?
   A. go   B. goes   C. to go

8. Fumiko _____ English at this school.
   A. study   B. studies   C. studys

9. Fumiko and Omar _____ students at this school.
   A. is   B. are   C. be

10. They _____ speak the same language.
   A. aren't   B. doesn't   C. don't

■ **EXERCISE 41—REVIEW:** Complete the sentences.

1. A: Do you _____?

   B: Yes, I do. How about you? Do you _____?

   A: _____.

2. A: _____ don't _____.
   B: I know.

3. A: _____ doesn't _____.

   B: Really? Does _____?
   A: I don't know.

4. A: Where is _____?
   B: At home.

   A: Where does _____?
   B: On Fifth Avenue.

5. A: _____?
   B: Yes, I do.

   A: _____?
   B: No, he doesn't.

   A: _____?
   B: Yes, I am.

   A: _____?
   B: No, he isn't.

6. A: Do you like _____?

   B: Yes, of course I _____. Everybody _____.

7. A: What _____ snakes?

   B: They _____ long, thin animals. They _____ have legs.

   A: _____ snakes reptiles?

   B: Yes, they _____.

   A: _____ snakes eat eggs?

   B: Yes, they _____.

8. A: _____ you usually _____ in the morning?

   B: _____.

   A: When _____?

   B: _____.

■ **EXERCISE 42—REVIEW:** Work in pairs. Follow the steps listed below.

1. STUDENT A: Say five things about Student B's physical appearance (for example, describe hair color, eye color, straight or curly hair, glasses, a mustache, a beard, etc.).
   STUDENT B: Agree or disagree with the description.

   Example:
   STUDENT A: You have dark hair.
   STUDENT B: *(Nods in agreement.)*
   STUDENT A: You have black eyes.
   STUDENT B: No, I have brown eyes.
   STUDENT A: You have dark brown eyes.
   STUDENT B: Okay. That's right.
   STUDENT A: You wear glasses.
   STUDENT B: Yes.
   Etc.

   Then switch roles, with Student B saying five things about Student A's appearance.

2. STUDENT A: Ask Student B five questions about things s/he has and doesn't have (for example, a car, a computer, a pet, children, a TV set, a briefcase, etc.).
   STUDENT B: Answer the questions.

   Example:
   STUDENT A: Do you have a car?
   STUDENT B: No.
   STUDENT A: Do you have a computer.
   STUDENT B: Yes, but it's not here. It's in my country.
   Etc.

Then switch roles.

   3. STUDENT A: Ask Student B five questions about things s/he likes and doesn't like (for example, kinds of food and drink, music, movies, books, etc.)
      STUDENT B: Answer the questions.

     Example:
     STUDENT A: Do you like pizza?
     STUDENT B: Yes.
     STUDENT A: Do you like the music of *(name of a group or singer)?*
     STUDENT B: No, I don't.
     Etc.

Then switch roles.

   4. Write about the other person. Give a physical description. Write about things this person has and doesn't have. Write about things this person likes and doesn't like.

■ **EXERCISE 43—REVIEW:** Find out information about your classmates' hometowns. Use the information to write a report. Ask questions about: *the name of the hometown, its location, its population, its weather and average temperature in a particular month (of your choosing).*

Example:
STUDENT A: What's your hometown?
STUDENT B: Athens.
STUDENT A: Where is it located?
STUDENT B: In southwestern Greece on the Aegean Sea.
STUDENT A: What's the population of Athens?
STUDENT B: 3,507,000.
STUDENT A: What's the weather like in Athens in May?
STUDENT B: It's mild. Sometimes it's a little rainy.
STUDENT A: What's the average temperature in May?
STUDENT B: The average temperature is around 8° Celsius.

Chart for recording information about your classmates' hometowns.

Name	*Spyros*			
Hometown	*Athens*			
Location	*SW Greece on Aegean Sea*			
Population	*almost 4 million*			
Weather	*mild in May (around 8°C, in the mid-forties Fahrenheit)*			

CHAPTER **3**

Expressing Present Time
(Part 2)

3-1 *BE + ING:* THE PRESENT PROGRESSIVE TENSE

am	+	*-ing*	(a) I ***am sitting*** in class right now.
is	+	*-ing*	(b) Rita ***is sitting*** in class right now.
are	+	*-ing*	(c) You ***are sitting*** in class right now.

In (a): When I say this sentence, I am in class. I am sitting. I am not standing. The action (sitting) is happening right now, and I am saying the sentence at the same time.

am, ***is***, ***are*** = helping verbs
sitting = the main verb

am, ***is***, ***are*** + ***-ing*** = the present progressive tense★

★The present progressive is also called the "present continuous" or the "continuous present."

■ **EXERCISE 1—ORAL (BOOKS CLOSED):** Practice using the PRESENT PROGRESSIVE by using *am/is/are + **wearing***.

PART I: Answer questions about what you are wearing today and what your classmates are wearing.

Example:
TEACHER: Rosa, what are you wearing today?
STUDENT: I'm wearing a white blouse and a blue skirt.
TEACHER: What is Jin Won wearing?
STUDENT: He's wearing blue jeans and a sweat shirt.
TEACHER: What color is his sweat shirt?
STUDENT: It's gray with red letters.
TEACHER: What else is Jin Won wearing?
STUDENT: He's wearing sneakers, white socks, and a wristwatch. Etc.

PART II: Identify who is wearing particular articles of clothing.

Example: a (blue) shirt
Response: Marco is wearing a blue shirt.

Example: (blue) shirts
Response: Marco and Abdul are wearing blue shirts.

Suggestions:

1. (gold) earrings	4. a (red) blouse	7. a (black) belt
2. blue jeans	5. (gray) slacks	8. a necklace
3. a blouse	6. (brown) boots	9. running shoes

■ **EXERCISE 2—ORAL:** What are the animals in the following pictures doing?

■ **EXERCISE 3—ORAL (BOOKS CLOSED):** Act out the directions. Describe the actions using the PRESENT PROGRESSIVE. Sustain the action during the description.

Example: Smile.
TEACHER: (Student A), please smile. What are you doing?
STUDENT A: I'm smiling.
TEACHER: (Student A) and (Student B), please smile. (Student A), what are you and (Student B) doing?
STUDENT A: We're smiling.
TEACHER: (Student C), what are (Student A and Student B) doing?
STUDENT C: They're smiling.
TEACHER: (Student A), please smile. (Student B), what is (Student A) doing?
STUDENT B: He/She is smiling.

1. Stand in the middle of the room.
2. Sit in the middle of the room.
3. Stand in the back of the room.
4. Smile.
5. Stand between (. . .) and (. . .).
6. Touch the floor.
7. Touch the ceiling.
8. Touch your toes.
9. Open/Close the door/window.
10. Close/Open the door/window.
11. Shake hands with (. . .).
12. Smile at (. . .).
13. Stand up and turn around in a circle.
14. Hold your book above your head.
15. Hold up your right hand.
16. Hold up your left hand.
17. Touch your right ear with your left hand.
18. Stand up.
19. Sit down.
20. Clap your hands.

■ **EXERCISE 4—ORAL (BOOKS CLOSED):** Practice using the PRESENT PROGRESSIVE by describing what your teacher and classmates are pantomiming, i.e., pretending to do. The pantomimist should sustain the action until the oral description is completed.

Example: drink
TEACHER: *(The teacher pantomimes drinking.)* What am I doing?
STUDENT: You're drinking.

Example: drive
TEACHER: (Student A), drive. Pretend to drive.
STUDENT A: *(The student pantomimes driving.)*
TEACHER: What are you doing?
STUDENT A: I'm driving.
TEACHER: What is (. . .) doing?
STUDENT B: He/She's driving.

1. eat
2. read
3. sleep
4. write
5. walk
6. run
7. fly
8. smile
9. laugh
10. cry
11. dance
12. wave
13. push
14. pull
15. clap
16. kick
17. count
18. stand in back of (. . .)
19. touch (. . .)
20. shake hands with (. . .)
21. sit on the floor

3-2 SPELLING OF -ING

	END OF VERB	→	-ING FORM
Rule 1:	A CONSONANT* + -e smile write	→ → →	DROP THE -e and ADD -ing smiling writing
Rule 2:	ONE VOWEL* + ONE CONSONANT sit run	→ → →	DOUBLE THE CONSONANT and ADD -ing** sitting running
Rule 3:	TWO VOWELS + ONE CONSONANT read rain	→ → →	ADD -ing; DO NOT DOUBLE THE CONSONANT reading raining
Rule 4:	TWO CONSONANTS stand push	→ → →	ADD -ing; DO NOT DOUBLE THE CONSONANT standing pushing

* Vowels = *a, e, i, o, u.*
    Consonants = *b, c, d, f, g, h, j, k, l, m, n, p, q, r, s, t, v, w, x, y, z.*
** Exception to Rule 2: Do not double *w, x,* and *y.*
    snow → snowing   fix → fixing   say → saying

■ **EXERCISE 5:** Write the **-ing** forms for the following words.

1. stand ____*standing*____

2. smile _____

3. run _____

4. rain _____

5. sleep _____

6. stop _____

7. write _____

8. eat _____

9. count _____

10. wear _____

11. ride _____

12. cut _____

13. dance _____

14. put _____

15. sneeze _____

16. plan _____

17. snow _____

18. fix _____

19. say _____

20. cry _____

■ **EXERCISE 6:** Write the *-ing* forms for the following words.

1. dream _____   6. hit _____

2. come _____   7. hurt _____

3. look _____   8. clap _____

4. take _____   9. keep _____

5. bite _____   10. camp _____

11. shine _____   16. pay _____

12. win _____   17. study _____

13. join _____   18. get _____

14. sign _____   19. wait _____

15. fly _____   20. write _____

■ **EXERCISE 7—ORAL:**   Practice using the PRESENT PROGRESSIVE to describe actions.

STUDENT A: Act out the given directions. Sustain the action until Student B's description is completed.

STUDENT B: Describe Student A's action using the present progressive.

Example: erase the board
STUDENT A: *(Student A sustains the action of erasing the board.)*
STUDENT B: (. . .)/He/She is erasing the board.

1. erase the board
2. draw a picture on the board
3. sneeze
4. cough
5. wave at your friends
6. sign your name on the board
7. clap your hands
8. walk around the room
9. count your fingers
10. bite your finger
11. hit your desk
12. drop your pen
13. tear a piece of paper
14. break a piece of chalk
15. fall down
16. sing, hum, or whistle
17. sleep
18. snore

19. chew gum
20. *(two students)* throw and catch *(something in the room)*
21. hold your grammar book between your feet
22. carry your book on the top of your head to the front of the room

■ **EXERCISE 8—WRITTEN (BOOKS CLOSED):** Practice spelling using *-ing.* As the teacher performs or pantomimes actions, write descriptions.

Example: wave
TEACHER: *(Acts out waving and asks, "What am I doing?")*
Written: **waving**

1. smile	5. stand	9. eat	13. drink
2. cry	6. sleep	10. run	14. sneeze
3. laugh	7. clap	11. sing	15. fly
4. sit	8. write	12. read	16. cut (a piece of paper)

3-3 THE PRESENT PROGRESSIVE: QUESTIONS

QUESTION	SHORT ANSWER + (LONG ANSWER)
	BE + SUBJECT + *-ING*
(a)	*Is* Mary *sleeping*	→ Yes, *she is.* (She's sleeping.) → No, *she's not.* (She's not sleeping.) → No, *she isn't.* (She isn't sleeping.)
(b)	*Are* you *watching* TV?	→ Yes, *I am.* (I'm watching TV.) → No, *I'm not.* (I'm not watching TV.)
	Q-WORD + *BE* + SUBJECT + *-ING*
(c) *Where* *is* Mary *sleeping?*	→ *On the sofa.* (She's sleeping on the sofa.)
(d) *Why* *are* you *watching* TV?	→ *Because I like this program.* (I'm watching TV because I like this program.)

■ **EXERCISE 9:** Make questions. Give short answers to yes/no questions.

1. A: What _____*are you writing?*_____
   B: A letter. (I'm writing a letter.)

2. A: _____*Is Ali reading a book?*_____

   B: No, _____*he isn't/he's not.*_____ (Ali isn't reading a book.)

3. A: _____

   B: Yes, _____ (Anna is eating lunch.)

4. A: Where _____
   B: At the Red Bird Cafe.   (She's eating lunch at the Red Bird Cafe.)

5. A: _____

   B: No, _____ (Mike isn't drinking a cup of coffee.)

6. A: What _____
   B: A cup of tea. (He's drinking a cup of tea.)

7. A: _____

   B: No, _____. (The girls aren't playing in the street.)

8. A: Where _____
   B: In the park. (They're playing in the park.)

9. A: Why _____
   B: Because they don't have school today. (They're playing in the park because they
      don't have school today.)

10. A: Hi, kids. _____

    B: No, _____. (We aren't drawing pictures with our crayons.)

    A: Oh? Then what _____
    B: Maps to our secret place in the woods. (We're drawing maps to our secret place in the woods.)

    A: Why _____
    Because we have a buried treasure at our secret place in the woods. (We're drawing maps because we have a buried treasure at our secret place in the woods.)

■ **EXERCISE 10—ORAL (BOOKS CLOSED):** Practice yes/no questions using the PRESENT PROGRESSIVE. The teacher will hand out slips of paper on which are written the directions in Exercise 4 on page 86.

STUDENT A: Pantomime the directions on your slip of paper.
STUDENT B: Ask Student A or another classmate a yes/no question using the present progressive.

Example: drive *(written on a slip of paper)*
STUDENT A: *(Student A pantomimes driving.)*
STUDENT B: Are you driving?
STUDENT A: Yes, I am.
          OR
STUDENT B: (Student C), is (Student A) driving?
STUDENT C: Yes, he/she is.

■ **EXERCISE 11:** Make questions with *where*, *why*, and *what*.

   1. A: _____*What are you writing?*_____
      B: A letter. (I'm writing a letter.)

   2. A: _____
      B: Because I'm happy. (I'm smiling because I'm happy.)

3. A: _____
   B: My grammar book. (I'm reading my grammar book.)

4. A: _____
   B: Because we're doing an exercise. (I'm reading my grammar book because we're doing an exercise.)

5. A: _____
   B: In the back of the room. (Roberto is sitting in the back of the room.)

6. A: _____
   B: Downtown. (I'm going downtown.)

7. A: _____
   B: Because I need to buy some shoes. (I'm going downtown because I need to buy some shoes.)

8. A: _____
   B: Blue jeans and a sweatshirt. (Akihiko is wearing blue jeans and a sweatshirt today.)

3-4 THE SIMPLE PRESENT vs. THE PRESENT PROGRESSIVE

STATEMENTS: (a) I **sit** in class *every day*. (b) I **am sitting** in class *right now*. (c) The teacher **writes** on the board on *every day*. (d) The teacher **is writing** on the board *right now*.	• The SIMPLE PRESENT expresses habits or usual activities, as in (a), (c), and (e). • The PRESENT PROGRESSIVE expresses actions that are happening right now, while the speaker is speaking, as in (b), (d), and (f).
QUESTIONS: (e) **Do** you **sit** in class every day? (f) **Are** you **sitting** in class right now? (g) **Does** the teacher **write** on the board every day? (h) **Is** the teacher **writing** on the board right now?	• The SIMPLE PRESENT uses **do** and **does** as helping verbs in questions. • The PRESENT PROGRESSIVE uses **am**, **is**, and **are** in questions.
NEGATIVES: (i) I **don't sit** in class every day. (j) I**'m not sitting** in class right now. (k) The teacher **doesn't write** on the board every day. (l) The teacher **isn't writing** on the board right now.	• The SIMPLE PRESENT uses **do** and **does** as helping verbs in negatives. • The PRESENT PROGRESSIVE uses **am**, **is**, and **are** in negatives.

■ **EXERCISE 12:** Complete the sentences with the words in parentheses.

1. I *(walk)* _____*walk*_____ to school every day. I *(take, not)*

   _____*don't take*_____ the bus.

2. I *(read)* _____ the newspaper every day. I *(read, not)*

   _____ my grammar book every day.

3. A: What *(you, read)* _____ right now?

   B: I *(read)* _____ my grammar book.

4. Robert *(cook)* _____ his own dinner every evening.

5. Right now Robert is in his kitchen. He *(cook)* _____ rice
   and beans for dinner.

6. Robert is a vegetarian. He *(eat, not)* _____ meat.

7. *(you, cook)* _____ your own dinner every day?

8. A: *(you, want)* _____ your coat?
   B: Yes.

   A: *(be, this)* _____ your coat?

   B: No, my coat *(hang)* _____ in the closet.

9. A: *(Tom, have)* _____ a black hat?
   B: Yes.

   A: *(he, wear)* _____ it every day?
   B: No.

   A: *(he, wear)* _____ it right now?

   B: I *(know, not)* _____. Why do you care about
   Tom's hat?

   A: I found a hat in my apartment. Someone left it there. I *(think)*

   _____ that it belongs to Tom.

10. Ahmed *(talk)* _____ to his classmates every day in class. Right now he

    (talk) _____ to Yoko.

11. Yoko and Ahmed *(sit)* _____ next to each other in class every day, so they

    often *(help)* _____ each other with their grammar exercises. Right now

    Yoko *(help)* _____ Ahmed with an exercise on present verb tenses.

12. It *(rain)* _____ a lot in this city, but it *(rain, not)*

_____ right now.   The sun *(shine)*

_____.   *(it, rain)* _____ a lot
in your hometown?

13. A: Hello?
    B: Hello. This is Mike. Is Tony there?
    A: Yes, but he can't come to the phone right now. He *(eat)*

    _____ dinner. Can he call you back in about ten minutes?
    B: Sure. Thanks. Bye.
    A: Bye.

14. Tony's family *(eat)* _____ dinner at the same time every day. During

    dinner time, Tony's mother *(let, not)* _____ the children talk
    on the phone.

15. A: What are you doing? *(you, work)* _____ on
        your English paper?

    B: No, I *(study, not)* _____. I *(write)*

        _____ a letter to my sister.

    A: *(you, write)* _____ to her often?

    B: I *(write, not)* _____ a lot of letters to anyone.

    A: *(she, write)* _____ to you often?

    B: Yes. I *(get)* _____ a letter from her about once a week. *(you, write)*

        _____ a lot of letters?

    A: Yes. I *(like)* _____ to write letters.

16. Olga Burns is a pilot for an airline company in Alaska. She *(fly)* _____

    almost every day. Today she *(fly)* _____ from Juno to Anchorage.

17. A: Where *(the teacher, stand, usually)* _____
        every day?

    B: She usually *(stand)* _____ in the front of the room every day.

    A: Where *(she, stand)* _____ today?

    B: She *(stand)* _____ in the middle of the room.

18. A: Excuse me. *(you, wait)* _____ for the downtown bus?

B: Yes, I *(be)* _____. Can I help you?

A: Yes. What time *(the bus, stop)* _____ here?
B: Ten thirty-five.

19. A: *(animals, dream)* _____?

B: I don't know. I suppose so. Animals *(be, not)* _____ very different from human beings in lots of ways.

A: Look at my dog. She *(sleep)* _____. Her eyes *(be)* _____ closed. At the same time, she *(yip)* _____ and *(move)* _____ her head and her front legs. I *(be)* _____ sure that she *(dream)* _____ right now. I'm sure that animals *(dream)* _____.

3-5 NONACTION VERBS NOT USED IN THE PRESENT PROGRESSIVE

(a) I'm hungry *right now*. **I want** an apple. (INCORRECT: *I am wanting an apple.*) (b) I **hear** a siren. **Do** you **hear** it too? (INCORRECT: *I'm hearing a siren. Are you hearing it too?*)	Some verbs are NOT used in the present progressive. They are called "nonaction verbs." In (a): *Want* is a nonaction verb. *Want* expresses a physical or emotional need, not an action. In (b): *Hear* is a nonaction verb. *Hear* expresses a sensory experience, not an action.

NONACTION VERBS		
want	hear	understand
need	see	know
like	smell	believe
love	taste	think (meaning *believe*)*
hate		

*Sometimes *think* is used in progressive tenses. See Chart 3-10 for a discussion of *think about* and *think that*.

■ **EXERCISE 13:** Use the words in parentheses to complete the sentences. Use the SIMPLE PRESENT or the PRESENT PROGRESSIVE.

1. Alice is in her room right now. She *(read)* _____*is reading*_____ a book.

   She *(like)* _____*likes*_____ the book.

2. It *(snow)* _____ right now. It's beautiful! I *(like)*

   _____ this weather.

3. I *(know)* _____ Jessica Jones. She's in my class.

4. The teacher *(talk)* _____ to us right now. I *(understand)*

   _____ everything she's saying.

5. Don is at a restaurant right now. He *(eat)* _____ dinner. He

   (like) _____ the food. It *(taste)* _____ good.

6. (Sniff-sniff). I *(smell)* _____ gas. *(you, smell)*

   _____ it too?

7. Jason *(tell)* _____ us a story right now. I *(believe)*

   _____ his story. I *(think)* _____ that his story is true.

8. Ugh! That cigar *(smell)* _____ terrible.

9. Look at the picture. Jane *(sit)* _____ in

   a chair. A cat *(sit)* _____ on her lap.

   Jane *(hate)* _____ the cat.

10. Look at the picture. Mr. Allen *(hold)*

    _____ a cat. He *(love)*

    _____ the cat. The cat *(lick)*

    _____ Mr. Allen's face.

3-6 SEE, LOOK AT, WATCH, HEAR, AND LISTEN TO

SEE, LOOK AT, and WATCH (a) I **see** many things in this room.	In (a): **see** = a nonaction verb. Seeing happens because my eyes are open. Seeing is a physical reaction, not a planned action.
(b) I**'m looking at** the clock. I want to know the time.	In (b): **look at** = an action verb. Looking is a planned or purposeful action. Looking happens for a reason.
(c) Bob **is watching** TV.	In (c): **watch** = an action verb. I *watch* something for a long time, but I *look at* something for a short time.
HEAR and LISTEN TO (d) I'm in my apartment. I'm trying to study. I **hear** music from the next apartment. The music is loud.	In (d): **hear** = a nonaction verb. Hearing is an unplanned act. It expresses a physical reaction.
(e) I'm in my apartment. I'm studying. I have a tape recorder. I**'m listening to** music. I like to listen to music when I study.	In (e): **listen (to)** = an action verb. Listening happens for a purpose.

■ **EXERCISE 14—ORAL:** Answer the questions.

1. What do you see in this room?
   Now look at something. What are you looking at?

2. Turn to page 85 of this book. What do you see?
   Now look at one thing on that page. What are you looking at?

3. Look at the floor. What do you see?

4. Look at the chalkboard. What do you see?

5. What programs do you like to watch on TV?

6. What sports do you like to watch?

7. What animals do you like to watch when you go to the zoo?

8. What do you hear right now?

9. What do you hear when you walk down the street?

10. What do you hear at night in the place where you live?

11. What do you listen to when you go to a concert?

12. What do you listen to when you go to a language laboratory?

3-7 NEED AND WANT + A NOUN OR AN INFINITIVE

	VERB	+	NOUN	Need is stronger than want. Need gives the idea that something is *very important*.
(a) We	**need**		**food**.	
(b) I	**want**		**a sandwich**.	Need and want are followed by a noun or by an infinitive.
	VERB	+	INFINITIVE	
(c) We	**need**		**to eat**.	An infinitive = **to** + the simple form of a verb.*
(d) I	**want**		**to eat** a sandwich.	

*The simple form of a verb = a verb without **-s**, **-ed**, or **-ing**.
Examples of the simple form of a verb: **come, help, answer, write**.
Examples of infinitives: **to come, to help, to answer, to write**.

■ **EXERCISE 15:** Use the words in the list or your own words to complete the sentences. Use an INFINITIVE (**to** + verb) in each sentence.

buy	*do*	*listen to*	*play*	*walk*
call	*get*	*marry*	*take*	*wash*
cash	*go*	*pay*	*talk to*	*watch*

1. Anna is sleepy. She wants _____*to go*_____ to bed.

2. I want _____ downtown today because I need

   _____ a new coat.

3. Mike wants _____ TV. There's a good program on Channel 5.

4. Do you want _____ soccer with us at the park this afternoon?

5. I need _____ Jennifer on the phone.

6. I want _____ to the bank because I need _____ a check.

7. James doesn't want _____ his homework tonight.

8. My clothes are dirty. I need _____ them.

9. John loves Mary. He wants _____ her.

10. David's desk is full of overdue bills. He needs _____ his bills.

11. It's a nice day. I don't want _____ the bus home today. I want

    _____ home instead.

12. Do you want _____ some music on the radio?

13. Helen needs _____ an English course.

14. Where do you want _____ for lunch?

■ **EXERCISE 16:** Here are ten short conversations. Complete the sentences. Use the words in parentheses and other necessary words.

1. A: *(go \ you \ want)* _____ *Do you want to go* _____ downtown this afternoon?

   B: Yes, I do. *(I \ buy \ need)* _____ *I need to buy* _____ a winter coat.

2. A: Where *(you \ go \ want)* _____ for dinner tonight?
   B: Rossini's Restaurant.

3. A: What time *(be \ need \ you)* _____ at the airport?
   B: Around six. My plane leaves at seven.

4. A: *(want not \ Jean \ go)* _____ to the baseball game.
   B: Why not?
   A: Because *(she \ need \ study)* _____ for a test.

5. A: I'm getting tired. *(take \ I \ want)* _____ a break for a few minutes.
   B: Okay. Let's take a break. We can finish the work later.

6. A: *(go back \ Peter \ want)* _____ to his apartment.
   B: Why?
   A: Because *(he \ want \ change)* _____ his clothes before he goes to the party.

7. A: *(come \ we \ need not)* _____ to class on Friday.
   B: Why not?
   A: It's a holiday.

8. A: Where *(you \ go \ want)* _____ for your vacation?
   B: *(I \ want \ visit)* _____ Niagara Falls, New York City, and Washington, D.C.

9. A: May I see your dictionary? *(I \ look up \ need)* _____ a word.
   B: Of course. Here it is.
   A: Thanks.

10. A: *(come \ want \ you)* _____ with us to the park?
    B: Sure. Thanks. *(I \ get \ need)* _____ some exercise.

3-8 WOULD LIKE

(a) I'm thirsty. I **want** a glass of water. (b) I'm thirsty. I **would like** a glass of water.	(a) and (b) have the same meaning, but **would like** is usually more polite than **want**. *I would like* is a nice way of saying *I want*.
(c) **I would like** **You would like** **She would like** **He would like** } a glass of water. **We would like** **They would like**	Notice in (c): There is not a final **-s** on **would**. There is not a final **-s** on **like**.
(d) CONTRACTIONS **I'd** = **I would** **you'd** = **you would** **she'd** = **she would** **he'd** = **he would** **we'd** = **we would** **they'd** = **they would**	**Would** is usually contracted to **'d** in speaking. Contractions of **would** and pronouns are often used in writing.
(e) WOULD LIKE + INFINITIVE I **would like** **to eat** a sandwich.	Notice in (e): **would like** can be followed by an infinitive.
(f) WOULD + SUBJECT + LIKE **Would** you **like** some tea?	In a question, **would** comes before the subject.
(g) Yes, I **would**. (I would like some tea.)	**Would** is used alone in short answers to questions with **would like**.

■ **EXERCISE 17—ORAL:** Change the sentences by using **would like**. Discuss the use of contracted speech with **would**.★

  1. Tony wants a cup of coffee.
     → *Tony would like a cup of coffee.*
  2. He wants some sugar in his coffee.
  3. Ahmed and Anita want some coffee, too.
  4. They want some sugar in their coffee, too.
  5. A: Do you want a cup of coffee?
     B: Yes, I do. Thank you.
  6. I want to thank you for your kindness and hospitality.
  7. My friends want to thank you, too.
  8. A: Does Robert want to ride with us?
     B: Yes, he does.

★**Would** is almost always contracted with pronouns in everyday speaking. The difference between *I'd like to go* and *I like to go* is sometimes difficult to hear. In addition, **would** is often contracted with nouns in speaking (but not in writing). There is a difference between *My friends'd like to come with us* and *My friends like to come with us*, but the difference is sometimes hard to hear.

■ **EXERCISE 18—ORAL (BOOKS CLOSED):** Answer the questions.

1. Who's hungry right now? (. . .), are you hungry? What would you like?
2. Who's thirsty? (. . .), are you thirsty? What would you like?
3. Who's sleepy? What would you like to do?
4. What would you like to do this weekend?
5. What would you like to do after class today?
6. What would you like to have for dinner tonight?
7. What countries would you like to visit?
8. What cities would you like to visit in *(the United States, Canada, etc.)*?
9. What languages would you like to learn?
10. You listened to your classmates. What would they like to do? Do you remember what they said?
11. Pretend that you are a host at a party at your home and your classmates are your guests. Ask them what they would like.
12. Think of something fun to do tonight or this weekend. Using *would you like*, invite a classmate to join you.

3-9 WOULD LIKE vs. LIKE

(a) I **would like to go** to the zoo. (b) I **like to go** to the zoo.	In (a): *I would like to go to the zoo* means *I want to go to the zoo.* In (b): *I like to go to the zoo* means *I enjoy the zoo.* **Would like** indicates that I want to do something now or in the future. **Like** indicates that I always, usually, or often enjoy something.

■ **EXERCISE 19—ORAL:** Answer the questions.

1. Do you like to go to the zoo?
2. Would you like to go to the zoo with me this afternoon?
3. Do you like apples?
4. Would you like an apple right now?
5. Do you like dogs?
6. Would you like to have a dog as a pet?
7. What do you like to do when you have free time?
8. What do you need to do this evening?
9. What would you like to do this evening?
10. What would you like to do in class tomorrow?

■ **EXERCISE 20:** Complete the sentences with your own words.

1. I need to _____ every day.

2. I want to _____ today.

3. I like to _____ every day.

4. I would like to _____ today.

5. I don't like to _____ every day.

6. I don't want to _____ today.

7. Do you like to _____?

8. Would you like to _____?

9. I need to _____ and

_____ today.

10. _____ would you like to _____ this evening?

3-10 THINK ABOUT AND THINK THAT

		THINK	+	ABOUT	+	A NOUN		In (a): Ideas about my family are in my mind every day.
(a)	I	think		about		my family every day.		
(b)	I am	thinking		about		grammar right now.		In (b): My mind is busy now. Ideas about grammar are in my mind right now.

		THINK	+	THAT	+	A STATEMENT		In (c): In my opinion, Sue is lazy. I believe that Sue is lazy.
(c)	I	think		that		Sue is lazy.		People use think that when they want to say (to state) their beliefs.
(d)	Sue	thinks		that		I am lazy.		The present progressive is often used with think about.
(e)	I	think		that		the weather is nice.		The present progressive is almost never used with think that. INCORRECT: I am thinking that Sue is lazy.

(f) I *think that* Mike is a nice person. (g) I *think* Mike is a nice person.	(f) and (g) have the same meaning. People often often omit *that* after *think*, especially in speaking.

■ **EXERCISE 21:** Use *I think (that)* to give your opinion.

1. English grammar is easy / hard / fun / interesting.

        I think (that) English grammar is . . . .

2. People in this city are friendly / unfriendly / kind / cold.

_____

3. The food at *(name of a place)* is delicious / terrible / good / excellent / awful.

_____

4. Baseball is interesting / boring / confusing / etc.

_____

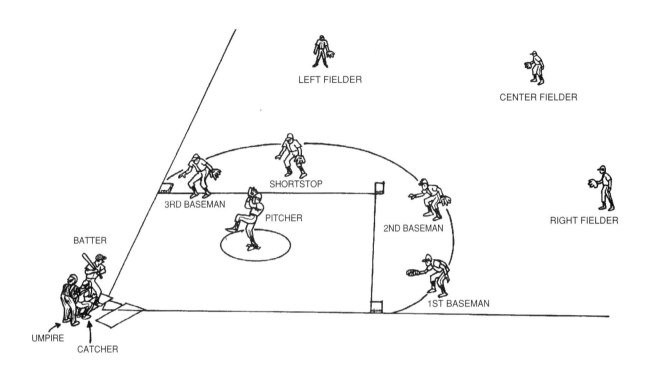

■ **EXERCISE 22:** Complete the sentences.

1. I think that the weather today is _____

2. I think my classmates are _____

3. Right now I'm thinking about _____

4. In my opinion, English grammar is _____

5. In my opinion, soccer is _____

6. I think that my parents are _____

7. I think this school _____

8. I think about _____

9. I think that _____

10. In my opinion, _____

■ **EXERCISE 23—ORAL:** State an opinion about each of the following topics.

> *Example:* books
> *Response:* I think that *War and Peace* is an excellent novel.
> In my opinion, *War and Peace* is an excellent novel.

1. this city
2. your English classes
3. music
4. movies
5. food
6. a current local, national, or international news story

■ **EXERCISE 24—REVIEW:** Complete the sentences. Use the words in parentheses. Use the SIMPLE PRESENT or the PRESENT PROGRESSIVE. Use an INFINITIVE where necessary.

the baby	= Bobby
the daughter	= Ellen
the son	= Paul
the mother	= Mrs. Smith
the father	= Mr. Smith
the cat	= Pussycat
the bird	= Tweetie
the mouse	= Mickey

(1)   The Smiths are at home. It is evening. Paul *(sit)* _____ on

(2)   the sofa. He *(read)* _____ a newspaper. Ellen *(sit)* _____

(3)   _____ at the desk. She *(study)* _____.

(4)   While she is studying, she *(listen to)* _____ music on her

(5)   radio. Paul *(hear)* _____ the music, but he *(listen to, not)* _____

(6)   _____ it right now. He *(concentrate)* _____

(7)   on the weather report in the newspaper. He *(think about)* _____

(8)   _____ the weather report.

(9)   Ellen *(study)* _____ her chemistry text. She *(like)* _____

(10)   _____ chemistry. She *(think)* _____ that chemistry is easy.

(11)   She *(think about)* _____ chemical formulas. She

(12)   *(understand)* _____ the formulas. She *(like)* _____

(13)   her chemistry course, but she *(like, not)* _____ her history course.

(14)   Mrs. Smith is in the kitchen. She *(cook)* _____ dinner.

(15)   She *(cut)* _____ up vegetables for a salad. Steam *(rise)*

(16)   _____ from the pot on the stove. Mrs. Smith *(like, not)*

(17)   _____ to cook, but she *(know)* _____ that her family

(18)   has to eat good food. While she *(make)* _____ dinner, Mrs. Smith

(19)   *(think about)* _____ a vacation on the beach. Sometimes

(20)   Mrs. Smith *(get)* _____ tired of cooking all the time, but she *(love)*

(21)   _____ her family very much and *(want)* _____ to take care

(22)   of their health. Her husband *(know, not)* _____ how to cook.

(23)   Mr. Smith *(stand)* _____ near the front door. He *(take, off)*

(24)   _____ his coat. Under his coat, he *(wear)* _____

(25)   _____ a suit. Mr. Smith is happy to be home. He *(think about)*

(26)   _____ dinner. After dinner, he *(want)*

(27)   _____ *(watch)* _____ television. He *(need)*

(28)   _____ *(go)* _____ to bed early tonight because he has a busy

(29)   day at work tomorrow.

(30)   In the corner of the living room, a mouse *(eat)* _____ a piece

(31)   of cheese. The mouse thinks that the cheese *(taste)* _____ good.

(32)   Pussycat *(see, not)* _____ the mouse. She *(smell, not)*

(33)   _____ the mouse. Pussycat *(sleep)* _____.

(34)   She *(dream about)* _____ a mouse.

(35)   Bobby is in the middle of the living room. He *(play)* _____

(36)   with a toy train. He *(see, not)* _____ the mouse because he

(37)   *(look at)* _____ his toy train. The bird, Tweetie, *(sing)*

(38)   _____ . Bobby *(listen to, not)* _____

(39) _____ the bird. Bobby is busy with his toy train. But Mrs.

(40) Smith can hear the bird. She *(like)* _____ *(listen to)*

(41) _____ Tweetie sing.

3-11   THERE + BE

THERE + BE + SUBJECT + LOCATION
(a) **There** **is** **a bird** in the tree.
 	
(b) **There** **are** **four birds** in the tree.
	There + **be** is used to say that something exists in a particular location.
	Notice: The subject follows **be:**
	  there + is + singular noun
	  there + are + plural noun	

(c) **There's** a bird in the tree.
 	
(d) **There're** four birds in the tree.
	Contractions:
	  there + is = there's
	  there + are = there're	

■ **EXERCISE 25:**   Complete the sentences with *is* or *are*.

1. There _____*is*_____ a grammar book on Ahmed's desk.

2. There _____*are*_____ many grammar books in this room.

3. There _____ two pens on Pierre's desk.

4. There _____ a pen on my desk.

5. There _____ thirty-one days in July.

6. There _____ only one student from Singapore in our class.

7. There _____ three students from Argentina.

8. There _____ ten sentences in this exercise.

9. There _____ a wonderful restaurant on 33rd Avenue.

10. There _____ many problems in the world today.

■ **EXERCISE 26—ORAL:** Make sentences with ***there is*** or ***there are***. Use the given phrases (groups of words) in your sentences.

1. a book \ on my desk
   → *There is (There's) a book on my desk.*

2. on Ali's desk \ some books
   → *There are (There're) some books on Ali's desk.*

3. on the wall \ a map

4. some pictures \ on the wall

5. in this room \ three windows

6. fifteen students \ in this room

7. in the refrigerator \ some milk

8. a bus stop \ at the corner of Main Street and 2nd Avenue

9. in Canada \ ten provinces

10. on television tonight \ a good program

■ **EXERCISE 27—ORAL:** After everybody puts one or two objects (e.g., a coin, some matches, a pen, a dictionary) on a table in the classroom, describe the items on the table by using ***there is*** and ***there are***.

Examples:
STUDENT A: There are three dictionaries on the table.
STUDENT B: There are some keys on the table.
STUDENT C: There is a pencil sharpener on the table.

■ **EXERCISE 28—ORAL/WRITTEN:** Describe your classroom. Use ***there is*** and ***there are***.

Example: I would like to describe this room. There are three windows.
There is a green chalkboard. Etc.

3-12 *THERE + BE*: YES/NO QUESTIONS

QUESTION		SHORT ANSWER
BE + *THERE* + SUBJECT		
(a) ***Is*** ***there*** ***any milk*** in the refrigerator?	→	*Yes, **there is**.*
	→	*No, **there isn't**.*
(b) ***Are*** ***there*** ***any eggs*** in the refrigerator?	→	*Yes, **there are**.*
	→	*No, **there aren't**.*

■ **EXERCISE 29—ORAL:** Ask a classmate a question about the contents of the refrigerator in the picture. Use the NOUNS in the list in your questions. Use "**Is there . . . ?**" or "**Are there . . . ?**"

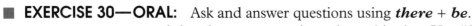

Example:
STUDENT A: Is there any milk in the refrigerator?
STUDENT B: Yes, there is.

Example:
STUDENT A: Are there any onions in the refrigerator?
STUDENT B: No, there aren't.

1. milk	6. bread	11. oranges
2. onions	7. apples	12. fruit
3. cheese	8. potatoes	13. meat
4. butter	9. orange juice	14. roses
5. eggs	10. strawberries	15. flour

■ **EXERCISE 30—ORAL:** Ask and answer questions using **there + be**.

STUDENT A: Ask a classmate questions about this city. Use "**Is there . . . ?**" or "**Are there . . . ?**" Your book is open.
STUDENT B: Answer the questions. Your book is closed.

Example:
STUDENT A: Is there a zoo in *(name of this city)*?
STUDENT B: Yes, there is. OR: No, there isn't. OR: I don't know.

1. a zoo	7. any good restaurants
2. an airport	8. a good (Vietnamese) restaurant
3. an aquarium	9. a botanical garden
4. any lakes	10. any swimming pools
5. a train station	11. an art museum
6. a subway	12. a good public transportation system

■ **EXERCISE 31—ORAL:** Complete the sentences with your own words.

Example: There . . . in this building.

Responses: There are five floors in this building.
There are many classrooms in this building.
There is an elevator in this building. Etc.

1. There . . . in this building.

2. There . . . in this city.

3. There . . . in my country.

4. There . . . in the world.

5. There . . . in the universe.

■ **EXERCISE 32—ORAL:** Ask and answer questions using ***there is/there are*** and an expression of location (e.g., in this city, in India, on First Street, etc.).

Example: any wild monkeys
STUDENT A: Are there any wild monkeys in New York City?
STUDENT B: No. There aren't any wild monkeys in New York City, but there are monkeys at the Bronx Zoo.

1. any elephants
2. any high mountains
3. a movie theater
4. a bookstore
5. any apartments for rent

6. any skyscrapers
7. any famous landmarks
8. any students from Indonesia
9. any red grammar books
10. an elevator

3-13 *THERE + BE:* ASKING QUESTIONS WITH *HOW MANY*

QUESTION		SHORT ANSWER + (LONG ANSWER)
HOW MANY + SUBJECT + *ARE* + *THERE* + LOCATION		
(a) ***How many chapters are there*** in this book?	→ →	Twelve. (There are twelve chapters in this book.)
(b) ***How many provinces are there*** in Canada?	→ →	Ten. (There are ten provinces in Canada.)

■ **EXERCISE 33—ORAL (BOOKS CLOSED):** Ask a classmate a question with ***how many***.

Example: days in a week
STUDENT A: How many days are there in a week?
STUDENT B: Seven. OR: There are seven days in a week.

1. pages in this book
2. chapters in this book
3. letters in the English alphabet
4. states in the United States
5. provinces in Canada

6. countries in North America
7. continents in the world
8. windows in this room
9. floors in this building
10. people in this room

■ **EXERCISE 34—ORAL:** Pair up with a classmate. Ask and answer questions about this room. Use ***how many***.

Example: desks
STUDENT A: How many desks are there in this room?
STUDENT B: Thirty-two. OR: There are thirty-two desks in this room.
STUDENT A: That's right. OR: No, I count thirty-three desks.

1. windows
2. doors
3. students

4. teachers
5. women
6. men

7. grammar books
8. dictionaries
9. etc.

■ **EXERCISE 35—ORAL:** Pair up with a classmate. Ask and answer questions about the
picture.

Examples:
STUDENT A: Are there any dogs in the picture?
STUDENT B: No, there aren't any dogs in the picture.
STUDENT A: Where are the boots?
STUDENT B: The boots are next to the picnic bench.
STUDENT A: How many trees are there?
STUDENT B: There's only one tree.

■ **EXERCISE 36—REVIEW:** Complete the sentences with your own words.

1. I need . . . because . . . .
2. I want . . . because . . . .
3. I would like . . . .
4. Would you like . . . ?
5. Do you like . . . ?
6. There is . . . .
7. There are . . . .
8. I'm listening to . . . , but I also hear . . . .
9. I'm looking at . . . , but I also see . . . .
10. I'm thinking about . . . .
11. I think that . . . .
12. In my opinion, ...
13. How many . . . are there . . . ?
14. Is there . . . ?

3-14 PREPOSITIONS OF LOCATION

(a) My book is **on** *my desk.*	In (a): *on* = a preposition *my desk* = object of the preposition *on my desk* = a prepositional phrase
(b) Tom lives **in** *the United States.* He lives **in** *New York City.* (c) He lives **on** *Hill Street.* (d) He lives **at** *4472 Hill Street.*	A person lives: **in** a country and **in** a city **on** a street, avenue, road, etc. **at** an address (See Chart 7-17 for more information about using **in** and **at**.)

SOME PREPOSITIONS OF LOCATION★

above	*far (away) from*	*inside*
around	*in*	*near*
at	*in back of*	*next to*
behind	*in the back of*	*on*
below	*in front of*	*on top of*
beside	*in the front of*	*outside*
between	*in the middle of*	*under*

★Prepositions of location are also called "prepositions of place."

A.

The book is **beside** the cup.
The book is **next to** the cup.
The book is **near** the cup.

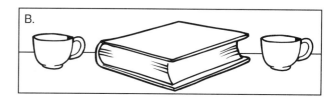

B.

The book is **between** two cups.

C.

In picture C, the book is **far away from** the cup.

D.

The cup is **on** the book.
The cup is **on top of** the book.

E.

The cup is **under** the book.

F.

The cup is **above** the book.

G.

A hand is **around** the cup.

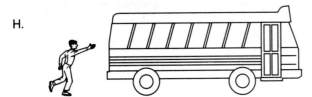

H.

The man is **in back of** the bus.
The man is **behind** the bus.

I.

The man is **in the back of** the bus.

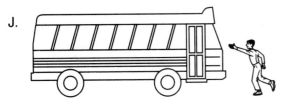

J.

The man is **in front of** the bus.
In H and J, the man is **outside** the bus.

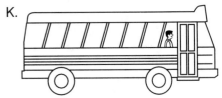

K.

The man is **in the front of** the bus.
In I and K, the man is **inside** the bus.

L.

The man is **in the middle of** the bus.

■ **EXERCISE 37:** Describe the pictures by completing the sentences with prepositional expressions of location. There may be more than one possible completion.

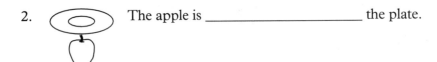

1. The apple is _____ *on, on top of* _____ the plate.

2. The apple is _____ the plate.

3. The apple is _____ the plate.

4. The apple is _____ the glass.

5.

The apple isn't near the glass. It is _____ the glass.

6.  The apple is _____ the glass.

7. 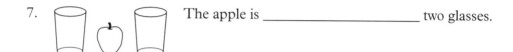 The apple is _____ two glasses.

8.  A hand is _____ the glass.

9.

The dog isn't inside the car. The dog is _____ the car.

10.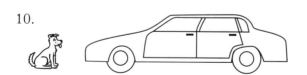

The dog is in _____ of the car.

11.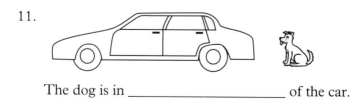

The dog is in _____ of the car.

12. The dog is in _____ of the car.

13. The dog is in _____ of the car.

■ **EXERCISE 38—ORAL:** Pair up with a classmate. Choose objects in the classroom (a book, a pen, an eraser, a cup, your hand, etc.) to demonstrate the meaning of the PREPOSITIONS in the list.

Example:
STUDENT A: Can you show me the meaning of "under"?
STUDENT B: Yes. The pen is under the book. Now it's your turn to demonstrate the meaning of "under."
STUDENT A: Okay. My hand is under this table.

1. under	7. in the middle of	13. in back of
2. above	8. around	14. in front of
3. next to	9. near	15. in the back of
4. between	10. far (away) from	16. in the front of
5. inside	11. behind	
6. on top of	12. below	

■ **EXERCISE 39:** Complete the sentences with *in*, *on*, or *at*.

1. Pablo lives _____ Canada.

2. He lives _____ Toronto.

3. He lives _____ Lake Street.

4. He lives _____ 5541 Lake Street _____ Toronto, Canada.

Complete the sentences:

5. I live _____. *(name of country)*

6. I live _____. *(name of city)*

7. I live _____. *(name of street)*

8. I live _____. *(address)*

■ **EXERCISE 40—REVIEW:** Below are some pictures of John and Mary.

A. VOCABULARY CHECKLIST

eat dinner	*a bowl*	*meat*
hold a knife and a fork	*a bowl of salad*	*a piece of meat*
have a steak for dinner	*a candle*	*a plate*
burn	*a cup*	*a restaurant*
	a cup of coffee	*a saucer*
	a fork	*a spoon*
	a glass	*a steak*
	a glass of water	*a table*
	a knife	*a waiter*
	a vase of flowers	

B. ANSWER THE QUESTIONS.

1. What is Mary doing?
2. What do you see on the table?
3. What is Mary holding in her right hand? in her left hand?
4. What is in the bowl?
5. What is on the plate?
6. What is in the cup?
7. What is burning?
8. Is Mary eating breakfast?
9. Is Mary at home? Where is she?
10. What is she cutting?

C. COMPLETE THE SENTENCES.

11. Mary is sitting _____ a table.

12. There is a candle _____ the table.

13. There is coffee _____ the cup.

14. Mary _____ holding a knife

    _____ her right hand.

15. She's _____ a restaurant.

16. She _____ at home.

17. She _____ eating breakfast.

A. VOCABULARY CHECKLIST

study at the library   *the circulation desk*
read a book   *a librarian*
take notes   *a shelf (singular)*
                         shelves (plural)★

B. ANSWER THE QUESTIONS.

1. What is John doing?
2. What do you see in the picture?
3. Is John at home? Where is he?
4. Is John reading a newspaper?
5. Where is the librarian standing?
6. Is John right-handed or left-handed?

C. COMPLETE THE SENTENCES.

7. John is studying _____ the library.

8. He is sitting _____ a table.

9. He is sitting _____ a chair.

10. His legs are _____ the table.

11. There are books _____ the shelves.

12. John is writing _____ a piece of paper.

13. He's taking notes _____ a piece of paper.

14. He _____ reading a newspaper.

15. The librarian _____ standing _____ the circulation desk.

16. Another student is sitting _____ John.

_____
★See Chart 4-5 for information about nouns with irregular plural forms.

A. VOCABULARY CHECKLIST

write a check★	*a bank*	*name and address*
sign a check	*cash*	*first name/given name*
sign her name	*a check*	*middle initial*
	the date	*last name/family name/surname*

B. ANSWER THE QUESTIONS.

1. What is Mary doing?
2. What is Mary's address?
3. What is Mary's full name?
4. What is Mary's middle initial?
5. What is Mary's last name?
6. How much money does Mary want?
7. What is in the upper left corner of the check?
8. What is in the lower left corner of the check?
9. What is the name of the bank?

C. COMPLETE THE SENTENCES.

10. Mary is writing a _____.

11. She is signing _____ name.

12. The name _____ the bank is First National Bank.

13. Mary lives _____ 3471 Tree Street.

14. Mary lives _____ Chicago, Illinois.

15. Mary's name and address are _____ the upper left corner _____ the check.

MARY S. JONES
3471 TREE ST.
CHICAGO, IL 60565

212

May 3 19 *95*

PAY TO THE
ORDER OF ___ *Cash* ___ $ *25 00*

Twenty five and 00/100 _____ DOLLARS

FIRST NATIONAL BANK
605 MICHIGAN AVE.
CHICAGO, IL 60503

Mary S. Jones

⑆021 200911 438 200

★*Check* (American English) is spelled *cheque* in British and Canadian English. The pronunciation of *check* and *cheque* is the same.

A. VOCABULARY CHECKLIST

cash a check	*a bank teller*	*a man (singular)*
stand in line	*a counter*	*men (plural)★*
	a line	*a woman (singular)*
		women (plural)★
		people (plural)★

B. ANSWER THE QUESTIONS.

1. What is Mary doing?
2. Is Mary at a store? Where is she?
3. What do you see in the picture?
4. Who is standing behind Mary, a man or a woman?
5. Who is standing at the end of the line, a man or a woman?

6. How many men are there in the picture?
7. How many women are there in the picture?
8. How many people are there in the picture?
9. How many people are standing in line?

C. COMPLETE THE SENTENCES.

10. Mary is _____ a bank.

11. Four people _____ standing in line.

12. Mary is standing _____ the counter.

13. The bank teller is standing _____ the counter.

14. A woman _____ standing _____ Mary.

15. Mary _____ standing _____ the end _____ the line.

16. A man _____ standing _____ the end _____ the line.

17. A businessman _____ standing _____ the woman with the big hat and the young man in jeans.

★See Chart 4-5 for information about nouns with irregular plural forms.

A. VOCABULARY CHECKLIST

cook	*a kitchen*	*bread*
cook dinner	*a list/a grocery list*	*coffee*
make dinner	*a pot*	*an egg*
taste (food)	*a refrigerator*	*butter*
	a stove	*milk*
	a pepper shaker	*pepper*
	a salt shaker	*salt*

B. ANSWER THE QUESTIONS.

1. What is John doing?
2. What do you see in the picture?
3. Where is John?
4. Is John tasting his dinner?
5. Is John a good cook?
6. Where is the refrigerator?
7. What is on the refrigerator?
8. Is the food on the stove hot or cold?
9. Is the food in the refrigerator hot or cold?

C. COMPLETE THE SENTENCES.

10. John is making dinner. He's _____ the kitchen.

11. There is a pot _____ the stove.

12. The stove is _____ the refrigerator.

13. There is a grocery list _____ the refrigerator door.

14. A salt shaker and a pepper shaker are _____ the stove.

15. There is hot food _____ top _____ the stove.

16. There is cold food _____ the refrigerator.

A. VOCABULARY CHECKLIST

watch TV / television	a cat	a living room
sit on a sofa	a dog	a rug
sing	a fish	a singer
sleep	a fishbowl	a sofa
swim	a floor	a TV set / a television set
	a lamp	

B. ANSWER THE QUESTIONS.

1. What are John and Mary doing?
2. What do you see in the picture?
3. Are Mary and John in a kitchen? Where are they?
4. Where is the lamp?
5. Where is the rug?
6. Where is the dog?
7. Where is the cat?
8. Is the cat walking? What is the cat doing?
9. What is the dog doing?
10. What is on top of the TV set?
11. Is the fish watching TV?
12. What is on the TV screen? What are John and Mary watching?

C. COMPLETE THE SENTENCES.

13. John and Mary _____ watching TV.

14. They _____ sitting _____ a sofa.

15. They _____ sleeping.

16. There is a rug _____ the floor.

17. A dog _____ sleeping _____ the rug.

18. A cat _____ sleeping _____ the sofa.

A. VOCABULARY CHECKLIST

talk to (someone)	*an arrow*	*a piece of paper*
talk on the phone	*a calendar*	*a telephone book*
talk to each other	*a heart*	*a wall*
smile	*a phone/a telephone*	
draw a picture	*a picture*	
	a picture of a mountain	

B. ANSWER THE QUESTIONS.

1. What are John and Mary doing?
2. What do you see in the picture?
3. Is John happy? Is Mary happy? Are John and Mary smiling?
4. Are they sad?
5. Who is standing? Who is sitting?
6. Is John in his bedroom? Where is John?
7. What is Mary drawing?
8. What is on Mary's table?
9. What is on the wall next to the refrigerator?
10. Where is the clock?
11. What time is it?
12. What is on the wall above the table?

C. COMPLETE THE SENTENCES.

14. John and Mary _____ talking _____ the phone.

15. John _____ talking _____ Mary. Mary _____ talking

    _____ John. They _____ talking to _____ other.

16. John is _____ the kitchen. He's standing _____ the refrigerator.

17. There is a calendar _____ the wall next to the refrigerator.

18. Mary _____ sitting _____ a table. She's _____ a picture.

19. There is a telephone book _____ the table.

20. There is picture _____ a mountain _____ the table.

A. VOCABULARY CHECKLIST

sleep	*a bed*
dream	*a dream*
dream about (someone/something)	*a head*
	a pillow

B. ANSWER THE QUESTIONS.

1. What is Mary doing?
2. What is John doing?
3. What are Mary and John doing?
4. What do you see in the picture?
5. Is Mary in her bedroom?
6. Is John in class? Where is he?
7. Is John standing or lying down?
8. Is Mary dreaming?
9. Are Mary and John dreaming about each other?
10. Are John and Mary in love?

C. COMPLETE THE SENTENCES.

11. John and Mary _____ sleeping. They are _____ bed.

12. John _____ dreaming _____ Mary. Mary _____ dreaming _____ John. They _____ dreaming _____ each other.

13. Mary's head is _____ a pillow.

14. John and Mary _____ in the living room.

15. They _____ asleep. They _____ awake.

16. John and Mary love each other. They are _____ love.

■ **EXERCISE 41—REVIEW:** Complete the sentences with the words in parentheses. Use the SIMPLE PRESENT or the PRESENT PROGRESSIVE.

1. I *(sit)* _____ *am sitting* _____ in class right now. I *(sit, always)*

_____ *always sit* _____ in the same seat every day.

2. Ali *(speak)* _____ Arabic, but right now he *(speak)*

_____ English.

3. Right now we *(do)* _____ an exercise in class. We *(do)*

_____ exercises in class every day.

4. I'm in class now. I *(look)* _____ at my classmates. Kim

(write) _____ in his book. Francisco *(look)*

_____ out the window. Yoko *(bite)* _____

her pencil. Abdullah *(smile)* _____. Maria *(sleep)*

_____. Jung-Po *(chew)* _____ gum.

5. The person on the bench in the picture below is Barbara. She's an accountant. She

(work) _____ for the government. She *(have)* _____

an hour for lunch every day. She *(eat, often)* _____ lunch in

the park. She *(bring, usually)* _____ a sandwich and

some fruit with her to the park. She *(sit, usually)* _____

on a bench, but sometimes she *(sit)* _____ on the grass. While she's at the

park, she *(watch)* _____ people and animals. She *(watch)*

_____ joggers and squirrels. She *(relax)* _____ when she eats at the park.

6. Right now I *(look)* _____ at a picture of Barbara. She *(be, not)* _____ at home in the picture. She *(be)* _____ at the park. She *(sit)* _____ on a bench. She *(eat)* _____ her lunch. Some joggers *(run)* _____ on a patch through the park. A squirrel *(sit)* _____ on the ground in front of Barbara. The squirrel *(eat)* _____ a nut. Barbara *(watch)* _____ the squirrel. She *(watch, always)* _____ squirrels when she eats lunch in the park. Some ducks *(swim)* _____ in the pond in the picture, and some birds *(fly)* _____ in the sky. A police officer *(ride)* _____ a horse. He *(ride)* _____ a horse through the park every day. Near Barbara, a family *(have)* _____ a picnic. They *(go)* _____ on a picnic every week.

■ **EXERCISE 42—ORAL:** Bring to class one or two pictures of your country (or any interesting picture). Ask your classmates to describe the picture(s).

■ **EXERCISE 43—WRITTEN:** Choose one of the pictures your classmates brought to class. Describe the picture in a composition.

■ **EXERCISE 44—REVIEW:** Choose the correct completion.

1. Jack lives _____ China.
   A. in
   B. at
   C. on

2. Anita and Pablo _____ TV right now.
   A. watch
   B. watching
   C. are watching

3. "_____ you writing a letter to your parents?"
   "No. I'm studying."
   A. Do
   B. Are
   C. Don't

4. I _____ like to write letters.
   A. no
   B. am not
   C. don't

5. "Jack has six telephones in his apartment."

   "I _____ you. No one needs six telephones in one apartment."
   A. am not believing   B. believe   C. don't believe

6. When I want to know the time, I _____ a clock.
   A. see   B. watch   C. look at

7. I need _____ a new notebook.
   A. buy   B. to buy   C. buying

8. "_____ a cup of tea?"
   "Yes, thank you."
   A. Would you like   B. Do you like   C. Like you

9. "Do you know Fatima?"

   "Yes, I do. I _____ she is a very nice person."
   A. am thinking   B. thinking   C. think

10. There _____ twenty-two desks in this room.
    A. be   B. is   C. are

11. Pilots sit _____ an airplane.
    A. in front of   B. in the front of   C. front of

12. I live _____ 6601 Fourth Avenue.
    A. in   B. on   C. at

■ EXERCISE 45—REVIEW: Correct the mistakes.

1. It's rainning today. I am needing my umbrella.

2. Do you want go downtown with me?

3. There's many problems in big cities today.

4. I like New York City. I am thinking that it is a wonderful city.

5. Does Abdul be sleeping right now?

6. Why you are going downtown today?

7. I'm listening you.

8. Are you hearing a noise outside the window?

9. I'd like see a movie tonight.

10. Kunio at a restaurant right now. He usually eat at home, but today he eatting dinner

    at a restaurant.

11. I am liking flowers. They are smelling good.

12. Mr. Rice woulds likes to have a cup of tea.

13. How many students there are in your class?

14. Alex is siting at his desk. He writting a letter.

15. Yoko and Ivan are study grammar right now. They want learn English.

16. Where do they are sitting today?

CHAPTER 4
Nouns and Pronouns

■ **EXERCISE 1:** Name things that belong to each category. Make a list. Compare your list with your classmates' lists. All of the words you use in this exercise are called "nouns."

1. Name clothing you see in this room. *(shirt)*
2. Name kinds of fruit. *(apple)*
3. Name things you drink. *(coffee)*
4. Name parts of the body. *(head)*
5. Name kinds of animals. *(horse)*
6. Name cities in the United States and Canada. *(New York, Montreal . . .)*
   NOTE: The names of cities begin with capital letters.
7. Name languages. *(English)* NOTE: The names of languages begin with capital letters.
8. Name school subjects. *(history)*

4-1 NOUNS: SUBJECTS AND OBJECTS

(a) NOUN **Birds** | fly. | subject verb	A NOUN is used as the **subject** of a sentence. A NOUN is used as the **object** of a verb.★ In (a): *Birds* is a NOUN. It is used as the subject of the sentence.
(b) NOUN NOUN **John** | is holding | a **pen**. | subject verb object	In (b): *pen* is a NOUN. It has the article *a* in front of it; *a pen* is used as the object of the verb *is holding*.
(c) NOUN NOUN **Birds** | fly | in | the **sky**. | subject verb prep. object of prep.	A NOUN is also used as the **object of a preposition.** In (c): *in* is a **preposition** (prep.). The noun *sky* (with the article *the* in front) is the OBJECT of the preposition *in*.
(c) NOUN NOUN NOUN **John** | is holding | a **pen** | in | his **hand**. | subject verb object prep. object of prep.	Examples of some common prepositions: *about, across, at, between, by, for, from, in, of, on, to, with.*

★Some verbs are followed by an object. These verbs are called transitive verbs (*v.t.* in a dictionary). Some verbs are not followed by an object. These verbs are called intransitive verbs (*v.i.* in a dictionary).

■ **EXERCISE 2:** Describe the grammatical structure of the sentences as shown in items 1 and 2. Then identify each NOUN. Is the noun used as:
- the subject of the sentence?
- the object of the verb?
- the object of a preposition?

1. Marie studies chemistry.

Marie	studies	chemistry	(none)	(none)
subject	verb	object	preposition	object of prep.

→ *Marie = a noun, subject of the sentence*
chemistry = a noun, object of the verb "studies"

2. The children are playing in the park.

The children	are playing	(none)	in	the park
subject	verb	object	preposition	object of prep.

→ *children = a noun, subject of the sentence*
park = a noun, object of the preposition, "in"

3. Children like candy.

subject	verb	object	preposition	object of prep.

4. The teacher is erasing the board with her hand.

subject	verb	object	preposition	object of prep.

5. Mike lives in Africa.

subject	verb	object	preposition	object of prep.

6. The sun is shining.

subject	verb	object	preposition	object of prep.

7. Robert is reading a book about butterflies.

subject	verb	object	preposition	object of prep.

8. Tom and Ann live with their parents.

subject	verb	object	preposition	object of prep.

9. Monkeys eat fruit and insects.

| subject | verb | object | preposition | object of prep. |

10. Mary and Bob help Sue with her homework.

| subject | verb | object | preposition | object of prep. |

11. Ships sail across the ocean.

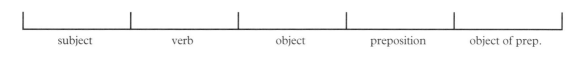

| subject | verb | object | preposition | object of prep. |

12. Water contains hydrogen and oxygen.

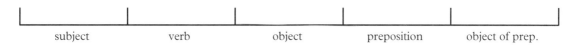

| subject | verb | object | preposition | object of prep. |

4-2 ADJECTIVE + NOUN

(a) I don't like ***cold*** *weather.* (adj) + (noun)	Adjectives describe nouns. In grammar, we say that adjectives "modify" nouns. The word "modify" means "change a little." Adjectives give a little different meaning to a noun: *cold weather, hot weather, nice weather, bad weather.*
(b) Alex is a ***happy*** *child.* (adj) + (noun)	
(c) The ***hungry*** *boy* has a ***fresh*** *apple.* (adj)+(noun) (adj) + (noun)	Adjectives come in front of nouns.
(d) The *weather* is ***cold.*** (noun) + (*be*) + (adj)	Reminder: An adjective can also follow ***be***; the adjective describes the subject of the sentence. (See Chart 1-6.)

COMMON ADJECTIVES

beautiful–ugly	*good–bad*	*angry*	*important*	**Nationalities**
big–little	*happy–sad*	*bright*	*intelligent*	*American*
big–small	*large–small*	*busy*	*interesting*	*Canadian*
cheap–expensive	*long–short*	*delicious*	*kind*	*Chinese*
clean–dirty	*noisy–quiet*	*famous*	*lazy*	*Egyptian*
cold–hot	*old–new*	*favorite*	*nervous*	*Indonesian*
dangerous–safe	*old–young*	*free*	*nice*	*Italian*
dry–wet	*poor–rich*	*fresh*	*ripe*	*Japanese*
easy–hard	*sour–sweet*	*honest*	*serious*	*Korean*
easy–difficult	*strong–weak*	*hungry*	*wonderful*	*Malaysian*
				Mexican
				Saudi Arabian

■ **EXERCISE 3:** Find the ADJECTIVES and NOUNS in the following sentences.

1. Jim has an expensive bicycle.
   → *Jim = a noun; expensive = an adjective; bicycle = a noun*
2. My sister has a beautiful house.
3. We often eat at an Italian restaurant.
4. Maria sings her favorite songs in the shower.
5. Olga likes American hamburgers.
6. You like sour apples, but I like sweet fruit.
7. Political leaders make important decisions.
8. Heavy traffic creates noisy streets.
9. Poverty causes serious problems in the world.
10. Young people have interesting ideas about modern music.

■ **EXERCISE 4:** Add ADJECTIVES to the sentences. Use any adjectives that make sense. Think of at least three possible adjectives to complete each sentence.

1. I don't like *cold / hot / wet / rainy / bad / etc.* weather.
2. Do you like _____ food?
3. I admire _____ people.
4. _____ people make me angry.
5. Pollution is a/an _____ problem in the modern world.
6. I had a/an _____ experience yesterday.

■ **EXERCISE 5:** Find each NOUN. Is the noun used as:
   • the subject of the sentence?
   • the object of the verb?
   • the object of a preposition?

1. <u>Bob</u> and his <u>wife</u> like <u>coffee</u> with their <u>breakfast</u>.
   → *Bob = a noun, used as a subject of the sentence*
   wife = a noun, used as a subject of the sentence
   coffee = a noun, object of the verb "like"
   breakfast = a noun, object of the preposition "with"

2. Jack doesn't have a radio in his car.

3. Monkeys and apes have thumbs.

4. Scientists don't agree on the origin of the earth.

5. Does Janet work in a large office?

6. Egypt has hot summers and mild winters.

7. Many Vietnamese farmers live in small villages near their fields.

8. Large cities face many serious problems.

9. These problems include poverty, pollution, and crime.

10. An hour consists of sixty minutes. Does a day consist of 1440 minutes?

4-3 SUBJECT PRONOUNS AND OBJECT PRONOUNS

SUBJECT PRONOUNS	OBJECT PRONOUNS	SUBJECT – OBJECT
(a) *I* speak English.	(b) Bob knows *me*.	*I* – *me*
(c) *You* speak English.	(d) Bob knows *you*.	*you* – *you*
(e) *She* speaks English.	(f) Bob knows *her*.	*she* – *her*
(g) *He* speaks English.	(h) Bob knows *him*.	*he* – *him*
(i) *It* starts at 8:00.	(j) Bob knows *it*.	*it* – *it*
(k) *We* speak English.	(l) Bob talks to *us*.	*we* – *us*
(m) *You* speak English.	(n) Bob talks to *you*.	*you* – *you*
(o) *They* speak English.	(p) Bob talks to *them*.	*they* – *them*

(q) I know **Tony**. **He** is a friendly person.	A pronoun has the same meaning as a noun. In (q): *he* has the same meaning as **Tony**. In (r): *him* has the same meaning as **Tony**. In grammar, we say that a pronoun "refers to" a noun. The pronouns *he* and *him* refer to the noun **Tony**.
(r) I like **Tony**. I know *him* well.	
(s) I have *a red book*. *It* is on my desk.	Sometimes a pronoun refers to a "noun phrase." In (s): *it* refers to the whole phrase *a red book*.

■ **EXERCISE 6:**   Complete the sentences. Use PRONOUNS (*I*, *me*, *he*, *him*, etc.).

1. Rita has a book. _____*She*_____ bought _____*it*_____ last week.

2. I know the new students, but Tony doesn't know _____ yet.

3. I wrote a letter, but I can't send _____ because I don't have a stamp.

4. Tom is in Canada. _____ is studying at a university.

5. Bill lives in my dorm. I eat breakfast with _____ every morning.

6. Ann is my neighbor. I talk to _____ every day. _____

   and _____ have interesting conversations together.

7. I have two pictures on my bedroom wall. I like _____.

   _____ are beautiful.

8. Ann and I have a dinner invitation. Mr. and Mrs. Brown want _____
   to come to dinner at their house.

9. Judy has a new car. _____ is a Toyota.

10. My husband and I have a new car. _____ got _____ last
    month.

■ **EXERCISE 7:**   Complete the sentences. Use PRONOUNS.

1. A: Do you know Kate and Jim?

   B: Yes, _____*I*_____ do. I live near _____*them*_____.

2. A: Is the chemical formula for water H_3O?

   B : No, _____ isn't. _____ is H_2O.

3. A: Would Judy and you like to come to the movie with us?

   B: Yes, _____ would. Judy and _____ would enjoy

   going to the movie with _____.

4. A: Do Mr. and Mrs. Kelly live in the city?

   B: No, _____ don't. _____ live in the suburbs. I

   visited _____ last month.

5. A: Do you know how to spell "Mississippi"?

   B: Sure! I can spell _____. _____ is easy to spell.

6. A: Is Paul Cook in your class?

B: Yes, _____ is. I sit next to _____.

7. A: Yoko and I are going to go downtown this afternoon. Do you want to come with _____?

B: I don't think so, but thanks anyway. Chris and _____ are going to go to the library. _____ need to study for our test.

8. A: Do you and Jack want to join me for dinner tonight at a Chinese restaurant?

B: Jack and _____ usually eat at home. _____ need to save our money.

A: _____ is not an expensive restaurant, and the food is really good.

B: Okay. Can you meet Jack and _____ there around six?
A: Great! See you then.

9. A: Do George and Mike come over to your house often?

B: Yes, _____ do. I invite _____ to my house often. We like to play cards together.
A: Who usually wins your card games?

B: Mike. _____ is a really good card player. We can't beat _____.

10. A: Hi, Ann. How do you like your new apartment?

B: _____ is very nice.

A: Do you have a roommate?

B: Yes. Maria Hall is my roommate. Do you know _____?

_____ is from Miami.

A: No, I don't know _____. Do you get along with _____?

B: Yes, _____ enjoy living together. You must visit

_____ sometime. Maybe _____ can come over for dinner sometime soon.

A: Thanks. I'd like that.

4-4 NOUNS: SINGULAR AND PLURAL

SINGULAR	PLURAL	
(a) **one pen** **one apple** **one cup** **one elephant**	**two pens** **three apples** **four cups** **five elephants**	To make the plural form of most nouns: add **-s**.
(b) **baby** **city**	**babies** **cities**	End of noun: *consonant* + **-y** Plural form: change **y** to **i**, add **-es**.
(c) **boy** **key**	**boys** **keys**	End of noun: *vowel* + **-y** Plural form: add **-s**.
(d) **wife** **thief**	**wives** **thieves**	End of noun: **-fe** or **-f** Plural form: change *f* to **v**, add **-es**.
(e) **dish** **match** **class** **box**	**dishes** **matches** **classes** **boxes**	End of noun: **-sh, -ch, -ss, -x** Plural form: add **-es**. Pronunciation: /əz/
(f) **tomato** **potato** **zoo** **radio**	**tomatoes** **potatoes** **zoos** **radios**	End of noun: *consonant* + **-o** Plural form: add **-es**. End of noun: *vowel* + **-o** Plural form add **-s**.

■ **EXERCISE 8:** Complete the sentences. Use the plural form of the words in the lists. Use each word only one time.

LIST A:

baby	cowboy	lady
✔ boy	dictionary	party
city	key	tray
country		

1. Mr. and Mrs. Parker have one daughter and two sons. They have one girl and two

   ___*boys*___.

2. The students in my class come from many _____.

3. Women give birth to _____.

4. My money and my _____ are in my pocket.

5. I know the names of many _____ in the United States and Canada.

6. I like to go to _____ because I like to meet and talk to people.

7. People carry their food on _____ at a cafeteria.

8. We always use our _____ when we write compositions.

9. Good evening, _____ and gentlemen.

10. _____ ride horses.

LIST B:

knife	*life*	*wife*
leaf	*thief*	

11. Please put the _____, forks, and spoons on the table.

12. Sue and Ann are married. They are _____. They have husbands.

13. We all have some problems in our _____.

14. Police officers catch _____.

15. It is fall. The _____ are falling from the trees.

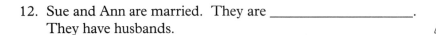

LIST C:

bush	*match*	*tax*
class	*potato*	*tomato*
dish	*sandwich*	*zoo*
glass	*sex*	

16. Bob drinks eight _____ of water every day.

17. There are two _____: male and female.

18. Please put the _____ and the silverware on the table.

19. All citizens pay money to the government every year. They pay their

    _____.

20. I can see trees and _____ outside the window.

21. I want to light the candles. I need some _____.

22. When I make a salad, I use lettuce and _____.

23. Sometimes Sue has a hamburger and French-fried _____ for dinner.

24. Some animals live all of their lives in _____.

25. Mehmet is a student. He likes his

    _____.

26. We often eat _____ for lunch.

■ **EXERCISE 9:** Practice the pronunciation of *-s/-es*.★

GROUP A: Final *-s* is pronounced /z/ after voiced sounds.

1. taxicabs
2. beds
3. dogs
4. balls
5. rooms
6. coins
7. years
8. lives
9. trees
10. cities
11. boys
12. days

GROUP B: Final *-s* is pronounced /s/ after voiceless sounds.

13. books
14. desks
15. cups
16. groups
17. cats
18. students

GROUP C: Final *-s/-es* is pronounced /əz/

• after "s" sounds:
19. classes
20. glasses
21. horses
22. places
23. sentences
24. faces
25. offices
26. pieces
27. boxes
28. sexes

• after "z" sounds:
29. sizes
30. exercises
31. roses
32. noises

• after "sh" sounds:
33. dishes
34. bushes

• after "ch" sounds:
35. matches
36. sandwiches

• after "ge/dge" sounds:
37. pages
38. ages
39. oranges
40. bridges
41. edges

★For more information, see Chart 2-8.

■ **EXERCISE 10:** Practice the pronunciation of *-s/-es*. Find the plural NOUN(S) in each sentence. Pronounce the noun(s). Then read the sentence aloud.

1. There are twenty desks in the room.

2. Oranges are usually sweet.

3. Roses are beautiful flowers. Rose bushes are beautiful.

4. The weather is terrible. It's raining cats and dogs.

5. We are reading sentences aloud.

6. I like to visit new places.

7. We do exercises in class.

8. I need two pieces of paper.

9. Don wants three sandwiches for lunch.

10. At the zoo you can see tigers, monkeys, birds, elephants, bears, and snakes.

11. Department stores sell many sizes of clothes.

12. The students are carrying books and bookbags.

13. The teachers have their offices in this building.

14. Engineers build bridges.

15. People have two ears, two eyes, two arms, two hands, two legs, and two feet.

16. Square tables and rectangular tables have four edges.

17. My dictionary has 350 pages.

18. I like apples, bananas, strawberries, and peaches.

19. There are three colleges in this city.

20. My apartment has cockroaches in the kitchen.

4-5 NOUNS: IRREGULAR PLURAL FORMS

SINGULAR	PLURAL	EXAMPLES
(a) *child*	**children**	Mr. Smith has one *child*. Mr. Cook has two **children**.
(b) *foot*	**feet**	I have a right *foot* and a left *foot*. I have two **feet**.
(c) *man*	**men**	I see a *man* on the street. I see two **men** on the street.
(d) *mouse*	**mice**	My cat sees a *mouse*. Cats like to catch **mice**.
(e) *tooth*	**teeth**	My *tooth* hurts. My **teeth** are white.
(f) *woman*	**women**	There's one *woman* in our class. There are ten **women** in your class.
(g) *fish*	**fish**	Bob has an aquarium. He has one *fish*. Sue has an aquarium. She has seven **fish**.
(h) *(none)**	**people**	There are fifteen **people** in this room. (Notice: *people* does not have a final **-s**.)

*****People** is always plural. It has no singular form.

■ **EXERCISE 11—ORAL (BOOKS CLOSED):** Use *two* and the plural form of the NOUN.

Example: one child
Response: two children

1. one child
2. one woman
3. one tooth
4. one foot
5. one man
6. one mouse
7. one fish
8. one page
9. one place
10. one banana
11. one child
12. one desk
13. one sentence
14. one man
15. one orange
16. one foot
17. one knife
18. one sex
19. one girl
20. one exercise
21. one tooth
22. one woman
23. one boy and one woman

■ **EXERCISE 12:** The object of the game on the following page is to fill in each list with NOUNS. Write one noun that begins with each letter of the alphabet if possible. The nouns must belong to the category of the list. When you finish one list, count the number of nouns in your list. That is your score.

List 1 Things in nature	List 2 Things you eat and drink	List 3 Animals and insects	List 4 Things for sale at *(name of a local store)*
A _____ air _____	A _____	A _____	A _____
B _____ bushes _____	B _____	B _____	B _____
C _____	C _____	C _____	C _____
D _____	D _____	D _____	D _____
E _____ earth _____	E _____	E _____	E _____
F _____ fish _____	F _____	F _____	F _____
G _____ grass _____	G _____	G _____	G _____
H _____	H _____	H _____	H _____
I _____ ice _____	I _____	I _____	I _____
J _____	J _____	J _____	J _____
K _____	K _____	K _____	K _____
L _____ leaves _____	L _____	L _____	L _____
M _____	M _____	M _____	M _____
N _____	N _____	N _____	N _____
O _____ oceans _____	O _____	O _____	O _____
P _____ plants _____	P _____	P _____	P _____
Q _____	Q _____	Q _____	Q _____
R _____ rain _____	R _____	R _____	R _____
S _____ stars _____	S _____	S _____	S _____
T _____ trees _____	T _____	T _____	T _____
U _____	U _____	U _____	U _____
V _____	V _____	V _____	V _____
W _____ water _____	W _____	W _____	W _____
X _____	X _____	X _____	X _____
Y _____	Y _____	Y _____	Y _____
Z _____	Z _____	Z _____	Z _____
Score: _____ 13 _____	Score: _____	Score: _____	Score: _____

4-6 NOUNS: COUNT AND NONCOUNT

	SINGULAR	PLURAL
COUNT NOUN	*a book* *one book*	*books* *two books* *some books* *a lot of books* *many books* *a few books*
NONCOUNT NOUN	*money* *some money* *a lot of money* (none) *much money* *a little money*	

A COUNT NOUN

SINGULAR:	PLURAL:
a + *noun* *one* + *noun*	*noun* + *-s*

A NONCOUNT NOUN

SINGULAR:	PLURAL:
Do not use *a*. Do not use *one*.	A noncount noun does not have a plural form.

COMMON NONCOUNT NOUNS

advice	mail	bread	pepper
furniture	money	cheese	rice
help	music	coffee	salt
homework	peace	food	soup
information	traffic	fruit	sugar
jewelry	weather	meat	tea
luck	work	milk	water

■ **EXERCISE 13:** Look at the italicized words. Underline the noun. Is the noun COUNT or NONCOUNT?

1. (COUNT)   NONCOUNT   He sits on *a chair*.

2. COUNT   (NONCOUNT)   He sits on *furniture*.

3. COUNT   NONCOUNT   She has *a coin*.

4. COUNT   NONCOUNT   She has *some money*.

5. COUNT   NONCOUNT   She has *some letters*.

6. COUNT   NONCOUNT   She has *some mail*.

7. COUNT   NONCOUNT   The street is full of *traffic*.

8. COUNT   NONCOUNT   There are *a lot of cars* in the street.

9. COUNT   NONCOUNT   I know *a fact* about bees.

10. COUNT   NONCOUNT   I have *some information* about bees.

11. COUNT   NONCOUNT   The teacher gives us *homework*.

12. COUNT	NONCOUNT	We have *an assignment*.
13. COUNT	NONCOUNT	I like *music*.
14. COUNT	NONCOUNT	Would you like *some coffee?*
15. COUNT	NONCOUNT	Our school has *a library*.
16. COUNT	NONCOUNT	People want *peace* in the world.
17. COUNT	NONCOUNT	I need *some advice*.
18. COUNT	NONCOUNT	Tom has *a good job*.
19. COUNT	NONCOUNT	He likes *his work*.
20. COUNT	NONCOUNT	Would you like *some water* with your food?
21. COUNT	NONCOUNT	Maria wears *a lot of jewelry*.
22. COUNT	NONCOUNT	She wears *earrings, rings, necklaces,* and *bracelets*.

■ **EXERCISE 14—ORAL:** Most nouns are COUNT NOUNS. Complete the following by naming things you see in the classroom.

1. I see a _____. I see a _____.

   I see a _____ and a _____.

2. I see two _____.

3. I see three / four / five / six / etc. _____.

4. I see some _____.

5. I see a lot of _____.

6. I see many _____.

4-7 USING AN vs. A

(a) **A** dog is **an a**nimal.	**A** and **an** are used in front of singular count nouns. In (a): *dog* and *animal* are singular count nouns.
(b) I work in **an o**ffice. (c) Mr. Lee is **an o**ld man.	Use **an** in front of words that begin with the vowels **a, e, i,** and **o**: *an apartment, an elephant, an idea, an ocean.* In (c): Notice that **an** is used because the adjective *(old)* begins with a vowel and comes in front of a singular count noun *(man).*
(d) I have **an** uncle. COMPARE: (e) He works at **a** university.	Use **an** if a word that begins with "*u*" has a vowel sound: *an uncle, an ugly picture.* Use **a** if a word that begins with "*u*" has a /yu/ sound: *a university, a usual event.*
(f) I nccd **an** hour to finish my work. COMPARE: (g) I live in **a** house. He lives in **a** hotel.	In some words that begin with "*h*," the "*h*" is not pronounced. Instead, the word begins with a vowel sound and **an** is used: *an hour, an honor.* In most words that begin with "*h*," the "*h*" is pronounced. Use **a** if the "*h*" is pronounced.

■ **EXERCISE 15:** Complete the sentences. Use **a** or **an**.

1. Bob is eating _____ apple.

2. Tom is eating _____ banana.

3. Alice works in _____ office.

4. I have _____ idea.

5. I have _____ good idea.

6. Sue is talking to _____ man.

7. Sue is talking to _____ old man.

8. I need to see _____ doctor.

9. Cuba is _____ island.

10. Mary is reading _____ article in the newspaper.

11. Bill is _____ uncle. He has _____ niece and two nephews.

12. _____ hour has sixty minutes.

13. _____ horse has hooves.

14. Miss Anderson has _____ job.

15. She has _____ unusual job.

16. _____ university is _____ educational institution.

■ **EXERCISE 16:** Complete the sentences. Use *a* or *an*.

1. Carol is _____ nurse.

2. I live in _____ apartment building.

3. I live in _____ noisy apartment building.

4. Jake has _____ honest face.

5. Does Mark own _____ horse?

6. A fly is _____ insect.

7. Sonya's English class lasts _____ hour.

8. I had _____ interesting experience.

9. My father has _____ office downtown. It's _____ insurance office.

10. Gary and Joel are having _____ argument in the cafeteria. It is _____ unpleasant situation.

11. Are you _____ responsible person?

12. _____ angry woman is complaining to the store's manager.

13. _____ healthy person gets regular exercise.

14. Janet is _____ honorable person.

15. My uncle Jake has never said _____ unkind word. He is _____ very special man.

4-8 USING *A/AN* vs. *SOME*

(a) I have *a* pen.	*A/An* is used in front of **singular** count nouns. In (a): the word *pen* is a singular count noun.
(b) I have *some* pens.	*Some* is used in front of **plural** count nouns. In (b): the word *pens* is a plural count noun.
(c) I have *some* rice.	*Some* is used in front of noncount nouns.* In (c): the word *rice* is a noncount noun.

*Reminder: Noncount nouns do not have a plural form. Noncount nouns are grammatically singular.

■ **EXERCISE 17:** Use *a/an* or *some* with the COUNT NOUNS in the following sentences. Are the nouns singular or plural?

1. Bob has _____*a*_____ book on his desk. → *book = a singular count noun*

2. Bob has _____*some*_____ books on his desk. → *books = a plural count noun*

3. I see _____ desk in this room.

4. I see _____ desks in this room.

5. Are _____ students standing in the front of the room?

6. Is _____ student standing in the middle of the room?

7. I'm hungry. I would like _____ apple.

8. The children are hungry. They would like _____ apples.

9. _____ children are playing in the street.

10. _____ child is playing in the street.

11. We are doing _____ exercise in class.

12. We are doing _____ exercises in class.

■ **EXERCISE 18:** Use *a*, *an*, or *some* with the nouns in the following sentences. Are they singular count nouns or noncount nouns?

1. I need _____*some*_____ money. → *money = a noncount noun*

2. I need _____*a*_____ dollar. → *dollar = a singular count noun*

3. Alice has _____ mail in her mailbox.

4. Alice has _____ letter in her mailbox.

5. I'm hungry. I would like _____ fruit.

6. I would like _____ apple.

7. Jane is hungry. She would like _____ food.

8. She would like _____ sandwich.

9. I'm thirsty. I'd like _____ water.

10. I'd like _____ glass of water.

11. Ann would like _____ milk.

12. I need _____ sugar for my coffee. Please hand me the sugar. Thanks.

13. I want to make _____ sandwich.

14. I need _____ bread and _____ cheese.

15. I'd like to have _____ soup with my sandwich.

■ **EXERCISE 19:** Use *a/an* or *some*.

1. Sonya is wearing _____*some*_____ silver jewelry. She's wearing

   _____*a*_____ necklace and _____*some*_____ earrings.

2. We have _____ table, _____ sofa, and

   _____ chairs in our living room.

3. We have _____ furniture in our living room.

4. Sue has a CD player. She is listening to _____ music.

5. I'm busy. I have _____ homework to do.

6. Jane is very busy. She has _____ work to do.

7. Jane has _____ job. She is _____ teacher.

8. I'm hungry. I would like _____ orange.

9. The children are hungry. They would like _____ oranges. They

   would like _____ fruit.

10. I need _____ information about the bus schedule.

11. I'm confused. I need _____ advice.

12. I'm looking out the window. I see _____ cars, _____

    bus, and _____ trucks on the street. I see _____ traffic.

13. Bob is having _____ beans, _____ meat, and

    _____ bowl of soup for dinner.

■ **EXERCISE 20:** Use the word in *italics* to complete the sentence. Add *-s* to a COUNT NOUN
   (or give the irregular plural form). Do not add *-s* to a NONCOUNT NOUN.

1. *money*   I need some _____*money*_____.

2. *desk*   I see some _____*desks*_____ in this room.

3. *man*   Some _____*men*_____ are working in the street.

4. *music* I want to listen to some _____.

5. *flower* Don wants to buy some _____ for his girlfriend.

6. *information* I need some _____.

7. *jewelry* Fred wants to buy some _____.

8. *furniture* We need to buy some _____.

9. *chair* We need to buy some _____.

10. *child* Some _____ are playing in the park.

11. *homework* I can't go to the movie because I have some _____ to do.

12. *advice* Could you please give me some _____?

13. *suggestion* I have some _____ for you.

14. *help* I need some _____ with my homework.

15 *tea* I'm thirsty. I would like some _____.

16. *food* I'm hungry. I would like some _____.

17. *sandwich* We're hungry. We want to make some _____.

18. *animal* I see some _____ in the picture.

19. *banana* The monkeys are hungry. They would like some _____.

20. *fruit*   I'm hungry.   I would like some _____.

21. *weather*   We're having some hot _____ right now.

22. *picture*   I have some _____ of my family in my wallet.

23. *rice, bean* I usually have some _____ and

                            _____ for dinner.

■ **EXERCISE 21:**   Change the italicized noun to its PLURAL FORM if possible, changing **a** to **some**. Make other changes in the sentence as necessary.

1. There is *a chair* in this room. PLURAL FORM → *There are some chairs in this room.*

2. There is *some furniture* in this room.   PLURAL FORM → *(none)*

3. I have *a coin* in my pocket.

4. I have *some money* in my wallet.

5. There is *some mail* in my mailbox.

6. There is *a letter* in my mailbox.

7. There's *a lot of traffic* on Main Street.

8. There's *a car* on Main Street.

9. Our teacher assigns *a lot of homework*.

10. I like rock *music*.

11. Hong Kong has hot *weather*.

12. I need *some information* and *some advice* from you.

13. There's *a dictionary* on the shelf.

14. I'd like to put *some cheese* on my *bread*.

15. I hope you do well on your exam. Good *luck!*

■ **EXERCISE 22—ORAL (BOOKS CLOSED):** Use *a*, *an*, or *some* with the given word.

Example: book   *Example:* books   *Example:* money
Response: a book   *Response:* some books   *Response:* some money

1. desk	14. apple	27. window	40. bread
2. desks	15. man	28. horse	41. office
3. animal	16. old man	29. hour	42. food
4. animals	17. men	30. dishes	43. table
5. chair	18. bananas	31. women	44. cheese
6. chairs	19. banana	32. oranges	45. matches
7. furniture	20. fruit	33. orange	46. adjective
8. child	21. island	34. place	47. advice
9. children	22. jewelry	35. places	48. house
10. music	23. university	36. water	49. people
11. homework	24. uncle	37. mail	50. potatoes
12. flower	25. rice	38. letter	51. potato
13. information	26. boys	39. letters	52. sugar

■ **EXERCISE 23:** Make the nouns PLURAL where necessary.

1. Toronto and Bangkok are big ~~city.~~ → *cities*

2. I need some information. → *(no change)*

3. Horse are large animals.

4. I like to listen to music when I study.

5. I have two small child.

6. I like to tell them story.

7. There are sixty minute in an hour.

8. Korea and Japan are country in Asia.

9. Children like to play with toy.

10. Our teacher gives us a lot of homework.

11. My bookcase has three shelf.

12. There are five woman and seven man in this class.

13. Bangkok has a lot of hot weather.

14. Are you hungry? Could I get you some food?

15. Taiwan and Cuba are island.

16. I drink eight glass of water every day.

17. Tomato are red when they are ripe.

18. There is a lot of traffic at five o'clock.

19. Before dinner, I put dish, spoon, fork, knife, and napkin on the table.

20. I have many friend. I don't have many enemy.

4-9 MEASUREMENTS WITH NONCOUNT NOUNS

(a) I'd like **some** *water*. (b) I'd like **a glass of** *water*. (c) I'd like **a cup of** *coffee*. (d) I'd like **a piece of** *fruit*.	Units of measure are used with noncount nouns to express a specific quantity, for example: *a glass of, a cup of, a piece of.* In (a): *some water* = an unspecific quantity. In (b): *a glass of water* = a specific quantity.

COMMON EXPRESSIONS OF MEASURE		
a bag of rice	*a bunch of bananas*	*a jar of pickles*
a bar of soap	*a can of corn*★	*a loaf of bread*
a bottle of beer	*a carton of milk*	*a piece of cheese*
a bowl of cereal	*a glass of water*	*a sheet of paper*
a box of candy	*a head of lettuce*	*a tube of toothpaste*

★In British English: *a tin of corn.*

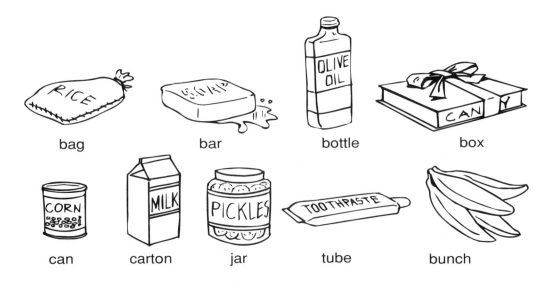

bag   bar   bottle   box

can   carton   jar   tube   bunch

■ **EXERCISE 24:** Complete the following. Use *a piece of*, *a cup of*, *a glass of*, or *a bowl of*.

You are hungry and thirsty. What would you like?

1. _____*a cup of / a glass of*_____ tea
2. _____ bread
3. _____ water
4. _____ coffee
5. _____ cheese
6. _____ soup
7. _____ meat
8. _____ wine
9. _____ fruit
10. _____ rice

■ **EXERCISE 25:** Complete the sentences with NOUNS.

1. At the store, I bought a carton of _____*orange juice / milk / etc.*_____

2. I also bought a tube of _____ and two bars of

    _____.

3. I got a can of _____ and a jar of _____.

4. I also got a loaf of _____ and a box of _____.

5. I wanted to get a head of _____, but none of it looked fresh.

6. I got a couple of bottles of _____ and a jar of _____.

■ **EXERCISE 26—ORAL (BOOKS CLOSED):** Use *I would like*. Use *a/an* or *some*.

Example: coffee
Response: I would like some coffee. OR: I would like a cup of coffee.

Example: new pen
Response: I'd like a new pen.

1. coffee	9. apple	17. sandwich	25. new shirt/blouse
2. money	10. oranges	18. meat	26. new shoes
3. dollar	11. water	19. roast beef	27. tea
4. paper	12. new pencil	20. soup	28. cheese
5. new book	13. information	21. salt	29. rice
6. new books	14. help	22. sugar	30. bread
7. fruit	15. advice	23. fish	31. chicken
8. banana	16. food	24. new car	32. new furniture

■ **EXERCISE 27—ORAL:** Change *a lot of* to *many* or *much* in the following sentences. Use *many* with COUNT NOUNS. Use *much* with NONCOUNT NOUNS.* (See Chart 4-6.)

1. I don't have a lot of money. → *I don't have much money.*

2. Tom has a lot of problems.

3. I want to visit a lot of cities in the United States and Canada.

4. I don't put a lot of sugar in my coffee.

5. I have a lot of questions to ask you.

6. Sue and John have a small apartment. They don't have a lot of furniture.

7. You can see a lot of people at the zoo on Sunday.

8. Dick doesn't get a lot of mail because he doesn't write a lot of letters.

9. Chicago has a lot of skyscrapers. Montreal has a lot of tall buildings too.

10. Mary is lazy. She doesn't do a lot of work.

11. I don't drink a lot of coffee.

12. Don is a friendly person. He has a lot of friends.

13. Do you usually buy a lot of fruit at the market?

14. Does Don drink a lot of coffee?

15. Do you write a lot of letters?

■ **EXERCISE 28:** Complete the questions with *many* or *much*.

1. How _____*much*_____ money do you have in your wallet?

2. How _____*many*_____ roommates do you have?

3. How _____ languages do you speak?

4. How _____ homework does your teacher usually assign?

5. How _____ tea do you drink in a day?

6. How _____ sugar do you put in your tea?

7. How _____ sentences are there in this exercise?

8. How _____ water is there in an Olympic-size swimming pool?

---

*Much is usually used only in negative sentences and in questions. *Much* is rarely used in statements.

■ **EXERCISE 29—ORAL:** Ask questions with ***how many*** or ***how much*** and ***are there*** or ***is there***.

Example: students in this room
Question: How many students are there in this room?

Example: coffee in that pot
Question: How much coffee is there in that pot?

1. restaurants in this city
2. desks in this room
3. furniture in this room
4. letters in your mailbox today
5. mail in your mailbox today
6. cheese in the refrigerator
7. bridges in this city
8. traffic on the street right now
9. cars on the street
10. people in this room

■ **EXERCISE 30:** Change ***some*** to ***a few*** or ***a little***. Use ***a few*** with COUNT NOUNS. Use ***a little*** with NONCOUNT NOUNS. (See Chart 4-6.)

1. I need some paper. → *I need a little paper.*

2. I usually add some salt to my food.

3. I have some questions to ask you.

4. Bob needs some help. He has some problems. He needs some advice.

5. I need to buy some clothes.

6. I have some homework to do tonight.

7. I usually get some mail every day.

8. I usually get some letters every day.

9. When I'm hungry in the evening, I usually eat some cheese.

10. We usually do some oral exercises in class every day.

■ **EXERCISE 31:** Use these words in the sentences. If necessary, use the plural form. Use each word only once.

bush	foot	information	page
child	fruit	knife	paper
city	furniture	✔ match	piece
country	help	money	sex
edge	homework	monkey	traffic

1. I want to light a candle. I need some _____*matches*_____.

2. I have a lot of _____ in my wallet. I'm rich.

3. There are two _____ : male and female.

4. I would like to visit many _____ in the United States. I'd like to visit Chicago, Los Angeles, Dallas, Miami, and some others.

5. There are some _____, forks, and spoons on the table.

6. I want to take the bus downtown, but I don't know the bus schedule. I need some

   _____ about the bus schedule.

7. I want to write a letter. I have a pen, but I need some _____.

8. There are three _____ in North America: Canada, the United States, and Mexico.

9. There are a lot of trees and _____ in the park.

10. Bob is studying. He has a lot of _____ to do.

11. I like to go to the zoo. I like to watch animals. I like to watch elephants, tigers, and

    _____.

12. There is a lot of _____ on the street during rush hour.

13. My dictionary has 437 _____.

14. This puzzle has 200 _____.

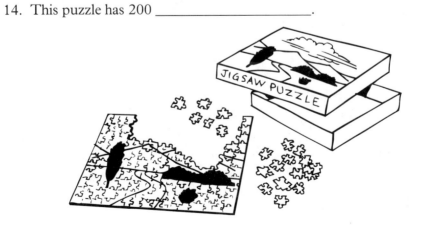

15. Barbara has four suitcases. She can't carry all of them. She

    needs some _____.

16. Susie and Bobby are seven years old. They aren't adults.

    They're _____.

17. A piece of paper has four _____.

18. We need a new bed, a new sofa, and some new chairs.

    We need some new _____.

19. People wear shoes on their _____.

20. I like apples, oranges, and bananas. I eat a lot of _____.

■ **EXERCISE 32:**   Use these words in the sentences. Use the plural form if necessary.

advice	*glass*	*potato*	*tray*
centimeter	*horse*	*sentence*	*valley*
dish	*inch*	*size*	*weather*
fish	*leaf*	*strawberry*	*woman*
foot	*man*	*thief*	*work*

1. _____ fall from the trees in autumn.

2. Sometimes I have a steak, a salad, and French-fried _____
   for dinner.

3. When the temperature is around $35°C$ ($77°F$), I'm comfortable. But I don't like

   very hot _____.

4. Cowboys ride _____.

5. Plates and bowls are called _____.

6. Married _____ are called wives.

7. _____ steal things: money, jewelry, cars, etc.

8. _____ are small, red, sweet, and delicious.

9. People carry their food on _____ at a cafeteria.

10. I'm not busy today. I don't have much _____ to do.

11. Sweaters in a store often have four _____ : small, medium,
    large, and extra large.

12. I have a problem. I need your help. I need some _____ from you.

13. Some _____ have mustaches.

14. Mountains are high, and _____ are low.

15. Ann has five _____ in her aquarium.

16. In some countries, people use cups for their tea. In other countries, they usually use

_____ for their tea.

17. There are 100 _____ in a meter.

18. There are 12 _____ in a foot.★

19. There are 3 _____ in a yard.★

20. There are twenty-five _____ in this exercise.

4-10 USING *THE*

(a) A: Where's David? B: He's in ***the*** *kitchen.*	A speaker uses ***the*** when the speaker and the listener have the same thing or person in mind. ***The*** shows that a noun is specific. In (a): Both A and B have the same kitchen in mind.
(b) A: I have two pieces of fruit for us, an apple and a banana. Which do you want? B: I'd like ***the*** *apple*, thank you.	In (b): When B says "the apple," both A and B have the same apple in mind.
(c) A: It's a nice summer day today. ***The*** *sky* is blue. ***The*** *sun* is hot. B: Yes, I really like summer.	In (c): Both A and B are thinking of the same sky (there is only one sky for them to think of) and the same sun (there is only one sun for them to think of).
(d) Mike has ***a*** *pen* and ***a*** *pencil.* ***The*** *pen* is blue. ***The*** *pencil* is yellow.	***The*** is used with: • singular count nouns, as in (d). • plural count nouns, as in (e). • noncount nouns, as in (f). In other words, ***the*** is used with each of the three kinds of nouns.
(e) Mike has ***some*** *pens* and *pencils.* ***The*** *pens* are blue. ***The*** *pencils* are yellow.	
(f) Mike has ***some*** *rice* and ***some*** *cheese.* ***The*** *rice* is white. ***The*** *cheese* is yellow.	Notice in the examples: the speaker is using ***the*** for the **second** mention of a noun. When the speaker mentions a noun for a second time, both the speaker and listener are now thinking about the same thing. First mention: I have ***a*** *pen.* Second mention: ***The*** *pen* is blue.

★1 inch = 2.54 centimeters. 1 foot = 30.48 centimeters. 1 yard = 0.91 meters.

■ **EXERCISE 33:** Complete the sentences with *the* or *a/an*.

1. I have _____ a _____ notebook and _____ grammar book. _____ notebook is brown. _____ grammar book is red.

2. Right now Pablo is sitting in class. He's sitting between _____ woman and _____ man. _____ woman is Graciela. _____ man is Mustafa.

3. Susan is wearing _____ ring and _____ necklace. _____ ring is on her left hand.

4. Tony and Sara are waiting for their plane to depart. Tony is reading _____ magazine. Sara is reading _____ newspaper. When Sara finishes _____ newspaper and Tony finishes _____ magazine, they will trade.

5. In the picture below, there are four figures: _____ circle, _____ triangle, _____ square, and _____ rectangle. _____ circle is next to _____ triangle. _____ square is between _____ triangle and _____ rectangle.

| circle | triangle | square | rectangle |

6. Linda and Anne live in _____ apartment in _____ old building. They like _____ apartment because it is big. _____ building is very old. It was built more than one hundred years ago.

7. I gave my friend _____ card and _____ flower for her birthday. _____ card wished her "Happy Birthday." She liked both _____ card and _____ flower.

8. We stayed at _____ hotel in New York. _____ hotel was very expensive.

■ **EXERCISE 34:** Complete the sentences with *the* or *a/an*.

(1)   A: Look at the picture on this page of your grammar book. What do you see?

(2)   B: I see _____ chair, _____ desk, _____ window, _____ plant.

(3)   A: Where is _____ chair?

(4)   B: _____ chair is under _____ window.

(5)   A: Where is _____ plant?

(6)   B: _____ plant is beside _____ chair.

(7)   A: Do you see any people?

(8)   B: Yes. I see _____ man and _____ woman. _____ man is

        standing. _____ woman is sitting down.

(9)   A: Do you see any animals?

(10) B: Yes. I see _____ dog, _____ cat, and _____ bird in _____

        cage.

(11) A: What is _____ dog doing?

(12) B: It's sleeping.

(13) A: How about _____ cat?

(14) B: _____ cat is watching _____ bird.

■ **EXERCISE 35:** Complete the sentences with *the* or *a/an*.

1. A: I need to go shopping. I need to buy _____ coat.

   B: I'll go with you. I need to get _____ umbrella.

2. A: Hi! Come in!

   B: Hi! _____ weather is terrible today! It's cold and wet outside.
   A: Well, it's warm in here.
   B: What should I do with my coat and umbrella?

   A: You can put _____ coat in that closet. I'll take _____ umbrella and

   put it in _____ kitchen where it can dry.

3. My cousin Jane has _____ good job. She works in _____ office. She

   uses _____ computer.

4. A: How much longer do you need to use _____ computer?
   B: Why?
   A: I need to use it too.
   B: Just five more minutes, then you can have it.

5. A: I need _____ stamp for this letter. Do you have one?
   B: Yes. Here.
   A: Thanks.

6. A: Would you like _____ egg for breakfast?

   B: No thanks. I'll just have _____ glass of juice and some toast.

7. A: Do you see my pen? I can't find it.

   B: There it is. It's on _____ floor.
   A: Oh. I see it. Thanks.

8. A: Be sure to look at _____ moon tonight.
   B: Why?

   A: _____ moon is full now, and it's beautiful.

9. A: Can I call you tonight?

   B: No. I don't have _____ telephone in my apartment yet. I just moved in
      yesterday.

10. A: Could you answer _____ telephone? Thanks.
    B: Hello?

4-11 USING Ø (NO ARTICLE) TO MAKE GENERALIZATIONS

(a) **Ø** *Apples* are good for you. (b) **Ø** *Students* use **Ø** *pens* and **Ø** *pencils*. (c) I like to listen to **Ø** *music*. (d) **Ø** *Rice* is good for you.	No article (symbolized by Ø) is used to make generalizations with: • plural count nouns, as in (a) and (b), and • noncount nouns, as in (c) and (d).
(e) Tom and Ann ate some fruit. **The** *apples* were very good, but **the** *bananas* were too ripe. (f) We went to a concert last night. **The** *music* was very good.	COMPARE: In (a), the word *apples* is general. It refers to all apples, any apples. No article (Ø) is used. In (e), the word *apples* is specific, so *the* is used in front of it. It refers to the specific apples that Tom and Ann ate. COMPARE: In (c), *music* is general. In (f), *the music* is specific.

■ **EXERCISE 36:** Complete the sentences with **the** or **Ø** (no article).

1. _____*Ø*_____ sugar is sweet.

2. Could you please pass me _____*the*_____ sugar?

3. Oranges are orange, and _____ bananas are yellow.

4. There was some fruit on the table. I didn't eat _____ bananas because they were soft and brown.

5. Everybody needs _____ food to live.

6. We ate at a good restaurant last night. _____ food was excellent.

7. _____ salt tastes salty, and _____ pepper tastes hot.

8. Could you please pass me _____ salt? Thanks. And could I have

   _____ pepper too?

9. _____ coffee is brown.

10. Steven made some coffee and some tea. _____ coffee was very good. I

    didn't taste _____ tea.

11. I like _____ fruit. I also like _____ vegetables.

12. There was some food on the table. The children ate _____ fruit, but they

    didn't want _____ vegetables.

13. _____ pages in this book are full of grammar exercises.

14. _____ books consist of _____ pages.

4-12 USING *SOME* AND *ANY*

STATEMENT:	(a) Alice has **some money**.	Use *some* in a statement.
NEGATIVE:	(b) Alice doesn't have **any money**.	Use *any* in a negative sentence.
QUESTION:	(c) Does Alice have **any money**? (d) Does Alice have **some money**?	Use either *some* or *any* in a question.

(e) I don't have **any money**. (noncount noun) (f) I don't have **any matches**. (plural count noun)	*Any* is used with noncount nouns and plural count nouns.

■ **EXERCISE 37:** Use **some** or **any** to complete the sentences.

1. Sue has _____*some*_____ money.

2. I don't have _____*any*_____ money.

3. Do you have _____*some/any*_____ money?

4. Do you need _____ help?

5. No, thank you. I don't need _____ help.

6. Ken needs _____ help.

7. Anita usually doesn't get _____ mail.

8. We don't have _____ fruit in the apartment. We don't have

   _____ apples, _____ bananas, or _____

   oranges.

9. The house is empty. There aren't _____ people in the house.

10. I need _____ paper. Do you have _____ paper?

11. Heidi can't write a letter because she doesn't have _____ paper.

12. Steve is getting along fine. He doesn't have _____ problems.

13. I need to go to the grocery store. I need to buy _____ food. Do you

    need to buy _____ groceries?

14. I'm not busy tonight. I don't have _____ homework to do.

15. I don't have _____ money in my purse.

16. There are _____ beautiful flowers in my garden this year.

Ask a classmate a question about what he or she sees in this room. Use *any* in the question.

Example: desks
STUDENT A: Do you see any desks in this room?
STUDENT B: Yes, I do. I see some desks / a lot of desks / twenty desks.

Example: monkeys
STUDENT A: Do you see any monkeys in this room?
STUDENT B: No, I don't. I don't see any monkeys.

1. books	6. food	11. hats	16. red sweaters
2. flowers	7. curtains	12. signs on the wall	17. dogs or cats
3. dictionaries	8. paper	13. bicycles	18. bookshelves
4. birds	9. bookbags	14. erasers	19. women
5. furniture	10. children	15. pillows	20. light bulbs

■ **EXERCISE 39:** Use *any* or *a*. Use *any* with NONCOUNT NOUNS and PLURAL COUNT NOUNS. Use *a* with SINGULAR COUNT NOUNS.

1. I don't have _____*any*_____ money.

2. I don't have _____*a*_____ pen.

3. I don't have _____*any*_____ brothers or sisters.

4. We don't need to buy _____ new furniture.

5. Mr. and Mrs. Kelly don't have _____ children.

6. I can't make _____ coffee. There isn't _____ coffee in the house.

7. Ann doesn't want _____ cup of coffee.

8. I don't like this room because there aren't _____ windows.

9. Amanda is very unhappy because she doesn't have _____ friends.

10. I don't need _____ help. I can finish my homework by myself.

11. I don't have _____ comfortable chair in my dormitory room.

12. I'm getting along fine. I don't have _____ problems.

13. Joe doesn't have _____ car, so he has to take the bus to school.

14. I don't have _____ homework to do tonight.

15. I don't need _____ new clothes.★

16. I don't need _____ new suit.

★*Clothes* is always plural. The word "clothes" does not have a singular form.

STATEMENT:	(a) Mary bought **something** at the store. (b) Jim talked to **someone** after class.	In a statement, use *something* or *someone*.
NEGATIVE:	(c) Mary didn't buy **anything** at the store. (d) Jim didn't talk to **anyone** after class.	In a negative sentence, use *anything* or *anyone*.
QUESTION:	(e) Did Mary buy **something** at the store? Did Mary buy **anything** at the store? (f) Did Jim talk to **someone** after class? Did Jim talk to **anyone** after class?	In a question, use either *something/someone* or *anything/anyone*.

■ **EXERCISE 40:** Complete the sentences. Use **something**, **someone**, **anything**, or **anyone**.*

1. I have _____ *something* _____ in my pocket.

2. Do you have _____ in your pocket?

3. Ken doesn't have _____ in his pocket.

4. I bought _____ when I went shopping yesterday.

5. Rosa didn't buy _____ when she went shopping.

6. Did you buy _____ when you went shopping?

7. My roommate is speaking to _____ on the phone.

8. Yuko didn't tell _____ her secret.

9. I talked to _____ at the phone company about my bill.

10. Did you talk to _____ about your problem?

11. Kim gave me _____ for my birthday.

12. Paul didn't give me _____ for my birthday.

13. Did Paul give you _____ for your birthday?

14. My brother is sitting at his desk. He's writing a letter to _____.

15. The hall is empty. I don't see _____.

_____

Someone and *somebody* have the same meaning. *Anyone* and *anybody* have the same meaning. You may also wish to include practice with *somebody* and *anybody* in this exercise.

16. A: Listen. Do you hear a noise?

    B: No, I don't. I don't hear _____.

17. A: Did you talk to Jim on the phone last night?

    B: No. I didn't talk to _____.

18. A: Where's your bicycle?

    B: _____ stole it.

19. A: Does _____ have some change? I need to use the pay phone.
    B: Here.
    A: Thanks. I'll pay you back later.

20. A: What did you do last weekend?

    B: I didn't do _____. I stayed home.

4-14 INDEFINITE PRONOUNS: *NOTHING* AND *NO ONE*

(a) I **didn't say anything**. (b) I **said nothing**.	(a) and (b) have the same meaning. *Anything* is used when the verb is negative. *Nothing* is used when the verb is affirmative.★
(c) Bob **didn't see anyone** at the park. (d) Bob **saw no one** at the park.	(c) and (d) have the same meaning. *Anyone* is used when the verb is negative. *No one* is used when the verb is affirmative.★

★INCORRECT: *I didn't say nothing.*
 INCORRECT: *Bob didn't see no one at the park.*

■ **EXERCISE 41:** Complete the sentences by using **anything**, **nothing**, **anyone**, or **no one**.

1. Jim doesn't know _____ about butterflies.

2. Jim knows _____ about butterflies.

3. Jean didn't tell _____ about her problem.

4. Jean told _____ about her problem.

5. There's _____ in my pocket. It's empty.

6. There isn't _____ in my pocket.

7. Liz went to a shoe store, but she didn't buy _____.

8. Liz bought _____ at the shoe store.

9. I got _____ in the mail today. My mailbox was empty.

10. George sat quietly in the corner. He didn't speak to _____.

11. The office is closed from 12:00 to 1:00. _____ is there during the lunch hour.

12. I know _____ about nuclear physics.

13. _____ was at home last night. Both my roommate and I were out.

14. Joan has a new apartment. She doesn't know _____ in her apartment building yet.

15. A: Do you know _____ about Iowa?

    B: Iowa? I know _____ about Iowa.
    A: It's an agricultural state that is located between the Mississippi and Missouri rivers.

■ **EXERCISE 42—REVIEW:** Describe the grammatical structure of the sentences as shown in item 1.

1. Mr. Cook is living in a hotel.

Mr. Cook	is living	(none)	in	a hotel
subject	verb	object	preposition	object of prep.

2. Anita carries her books in her bookbag.

subject	verb	object	preposition	object of prep.

3. Snow falls.

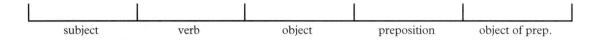

| subject | verb | object | preposition | object of prep. |

4. Monkeys sleep in trees.

| subject | verb | object | preposition | object of prep. |

5. The teacher is writing words on the chalkboard.

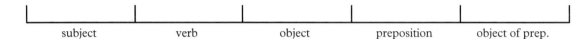

| subject | verb | object | preposition | object of prep. |

6. I like apples.

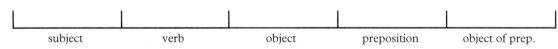

| subject | verb | object | preposition | object of prep. |

■ **EXERCISE 43—REVIEW:** A *complete sentence* has a subject and a verb. An *incomplete sentence* is a group of words that does not have a subject and a verb.
> If the words are a complete sentence, change the first letter to a capital letter (a big letter) and add final punctuation (a period or a question mark). If the words are an incomplete sentence, write "*Inc.*" to mean "*Incomplete.*"

1. monkeys like bananas → *M͟monkeys like bananas.*

2. in my garden → *Inc.*

3. do you like sour apples → *D͟o you like sour apples?*

4. rain falls

5. teaches English

6. this class ends at two o'clock

7. do the students go to class on Saturdays

8. in the classroom

9. my mother works in an office

10. my father to foreign countries on business every month

11. in Spain this month

12. does your brother have a job

13. does not work

14. where do you work

15. my brother lives in an apartment

16. has a roommate

17. the apartment has two bedrooms

18. a small kitchen and a big living room

19. on the third floor

20. pays the rent on the first day of every month

■ **EXERCISE 44—REVIEW:** Choose the correct completion.

1. My sister and I live together. Our parents call _____*A*_____ on the telephone often.
   A. us   B. them   C. we   D. they

2. Tom has a broken leg. I visit _____ in the hospital every day.
   A. he   B. him   C. them   D. it

3. Sue and I are good friends. _____ spend a lot of time together.
   A. They   B. You   C. We   D. She

4. Our children enjoy the zoo. We take _____ to the zoo often.
   A. it   B. they   C. them   D. him

5. Mary drives an old car. She takes good care of _____.
   A. her   B. them   C. it   D. him

6. Jack and _____ don't know Mr. Bush.
   A. I   B. me   C. us   D. them

7. Ms. Gray is a lawyer in Chicago. Do you know _____?
   A. them   B. it   C. him   D. her

8. Ahmed lives near Yoko and _____.
   A. I   B. me   C. him   D. her

9. My sister and a friend are visiting me. _____ are visiting here for two days.
   A. She   B. They   C. We   D. Them

10. Do _____ have the correct time?
   A. you   B. them   C. him   D. her

■ EXERCISE 45—REVIEW: Correct the errors in the following.

1. Omar a car has. → *Omar has a car.*

2. Our teacher gives tests difficult.

3. I need an advice from you.

4. Alex helps Mike and I.

5. I like rock musics. I listen to them every day.

6. Babys cry.

7. Mike and Tom in an apartment live.

8. There are seven woman in this class.

9. I don't like hot weathers.

10. I usually have a egg for breakfast.

11. There are nineteen peoples in my class.

12. Sun rises every morning.

13. Olga and Ivan has three childrens.

14. The students in this class do a lot of homeworks every day.

15. How many language do you know?

16. I don't have many money.

17. There is twenty classroom in this building.

18. I don't know nothing about ancient history.

■ **EXERCISE 46—REVIEW:** In pairs, pretend that tomorrow you are moving into a new apartment together. What do you need? Ask each other questions. Discuss your needs.

In writing, list the things you need and indicate quantity (*two, some, a lot of, a little, etc.*). List twenty to thirty things. Be sure to write down the <u>quantity</u>. You are completing this sentence: "*We need . . . .*"

Example: We need . . .
1. a sofa.
2. two beds.
3. a can opener.
4. some spaghetti.
5. a little fruit.
6. some bookcases. etc.

■ **EXERCISE 47—REVIEW:** Make a list of everything in the picture by completing the sentence "*I see . . . .*" Try to use numbers (e.g., *three* spoons) or other units of measure (e.g., *a box of* candy). Use *a* for singular count nouns (e.g., *a fly*).

Example: I see three spoons, a box of candy, a fly, etc.

■ **EXERCISE 48—REVIEW:** In pairs, ask and answer questions about the things and people in the picture on the following page.

Example:
STUDENT A: How many boys are there in the picture?
STUDENT B: There are three boys in the picture.
STUDENT A: Are there any flowers?
STUDENT B: No, there aren't any flowers in the picture.
STUDENT A: Are you sure?
STUDENT B: Well, hmmm. I don't see any flowers.
STUDENT A: Oh?

CHAPTER **5**

Expressing Past Time

5-1 USING *BE*: PAST TIME

PRESENT TIME	PAST TIME
(a) I **am** in class **today.** (c) Alice **is** at the library **today**. (e) My friends **are** at home **today.**	(b) I **was** in class **yesterday**. (d) Alice **was** at the library **yesterday.** (f) My friends **were** at home **yesterday**.

SIMPLE PAST TENSE OF *BE*		
Singular **I was** **you were** (one person) **she was** **he was** **it was**	*Plural* **we were** **you were** (more than one person) **they were**	$\left.\begin{array}{l} I \\ she \\ he \\ it \end{array}\right\}$ + *was* $\left.\begin{array}{l} we \\ you \\ they \end{array}\right\}$ + *were*

■ **EXERCISE 1—ORAL:**   Change the sentences to the past.

1. Bob is in class today. → *He was in class yesterday too.*

2. I'm in class today. → *I was in class yesterday too.*

3. Mary is at the library today.

4. We're in class today.

5. You're busy today.

6. I'm happy today.

7. The classroom is hot today.

8. Ann is in her office today.

9. Tom is in his office today.

10. Ann and Tom are in their offices today.

■ **EXERCISE 2—ORAL (BOOKS CLOSED):**   Talk about today and yesterday.

> *Example:*   I'm in class.
> *Response:*   I'm in class **today**. I was in class **yesterday too**.
> *Example:*   (. . .) is in class.
> *Response:*   (. . .) is in class **today**. She/He was in class **yesterday too**.

1. We're in class.
2. I'm in class.
3. (. . .) is in class
4. (. . .) and (. . .) are in class.
5. (. . .) is here.

6. (. . .) is absent.
7. I'm tired.
8. (. . .) and (. . .) are (in the front row).
9. The door is open/closed.
10. It's hot/cold.

5-2   PAST OF *BE:* NEGATIVE

(a) I **was not** in class yesterday.	NEGATIVE CONTRACTIONS:	**was** + **not** = **wasn't** **were** + **not** = **weren't**
(b) I **wasn't** in class yesterday.		

(c) They **were not** at home last night. (d) They **weren't** at home last night.	$\left.\begin{array}{l}I\\she\\he\\it\end{array}\right\}$ + *wasn't* $\left.\begin{array}{l}we\\you\\they\end{array}\right\}$ + *weren't*

■ **EXERCISE 3:**   Study the time expressions. Then complete the sentences. Use **wasn't** or **weren't**. Use a past time expression.

PRESENT		PAST
today	→	yesterday
this morning	→	yesterday morning
this afternoon	→	yesterday afternoon
tonight	→	last night
this week	→	last week

1. Ken is here today, but _____ *he wasn't here yesterday.* _____

2. I'm at home tonight, but _____ *I wasn't at home last night.* _____

3. Olga is busy today, but _____

4. We're in class this morning, but _____

5. Tom is at the library tonight, but _____

6. It's cold this week, but _____

7. Alex and Rita are at work this afternoon, but _____

8. Mr. and Mrs. Jones are at home tonight, but _____

9. You're in class today, but _____

10. Dr. Ruckman is in her office this afternoon, but _____

5-3 PAST OF *BE:* QUESTIONS

YES/NO QUESTIONS	SHORT ANSWER + (LONG ANSWER)
(a) ***Were you*** in class yesterday? *(be)* + (subject)	→ ***Yes, I was.*** (I was in class yesterday.) → ***No, I wasn't.*** (I wasn't in class yesterday.)
(b) ***Was Carlos*** at home last night? *(be)* + (subject)	→ ***Yes, he was.*** (He was at home last night.) → ***No, he wasn't.*** (He wasn't at home last night.)
INFORMATION QUESTIONS	SHORT ANSWER + (LONG ANSWER)
(c) ***Where were you*** yesterday? *Where* + *(be)* + (subject)	→ ***In class.*** (I was in class yesterday.)
(d) ***Where was Jennifer*** last night? *Where* + *(be)* + (subject)	→ ***At home.*** (She was at home last night.)

■ **EXERCISE 4:** Make questions and give short answers.

1. *(you \ at home \ last night)*

   A: ____*Were you at home last night?*_____

   B: No, ____*I wasn't.*_____

2. *(Mr. Yamamoto \ absent from class \ yesterday)*

   A: _____

   B: Yes, _____

3. *(Alex and Sue \ at home \ last night)*

   A: _____

   B: Yes, _____

4. *(you \ nervous \ the first day of class)*

   A: _____

   B: No, _____

5. *(Ahmed \ at the library \ last night)*

A: _____

B: Yes, _____

6. *(Mr. Shin \ in class \ yesterday)*

A: _____

B: No, _____

A: Where _____

B: At home.

7. *(you and your wife \ in Canada \ last year)*

A: _____

B: No, _____

A: Where _____

B: In Ireland.

■ **EXERCISE 5:** Make questions and give short answers.

1. *(you \ in class \ yesterday)*

A: ___*Were you in class yesterday?*_____

B: Yes, ___*I was.*_____

2. *(Anita \ in class \ today)*

A: ___*Is Anita in class today?*_____

B: No, ___*she isn't.*_____ She's absent.

3. *(you \ tired \ last night)*

A: _____

B: Yes, _____. I went to bed early.

4. *(you \ hungry \ right now)*

A: _____

B: No, _____, but I'm thirsty.

5. *(the weather \ hot in New York City \ last summer)*

    A: _____

    B: Yes, _____. It was very hot.

6. *(the weather \ cold in Alaska \ in the winter)*

    A: _____

    B: Yes, _____. It's very cold.

7. *(Yoko and Mohammed \ here \ yesterday afternoon)*

    A: _____

    B: Yes, _____

8. *(the students in this class \ intelligent)*

    A: _____

    B: Of course _____! They are very intelligent!

9. *(Mr. Tok \ absent \ today)*

    A: _____

    B: Yes, _____

    A: Where _____

    B: _____

10. *(Tony and Benito \ at the party \ last night)*

    A: _____

    B: No, _____

    A: Where _____

    B: _____

11. *(Mr. and Mrs. Rice \ in town \ this week)*

    A: _____

    B: No, _____. They're out of town.

    A: Oh? Where _____

    B: _____

12. *(Anna \ out of town \ last week)*

A: _____

B: Yes, _____

A: Where _____

B: _____

■ **EXERCISE 6—ORAL (BOOKS CLOSED):** Pair up with a classmate and ask questions. If Student B answers ***yes,*** the exercise item is finished. If Student B answers ***no,*** Student A should follow with a ***where***-question.

Example: in class \ now
STUDENT A: (. . .), are you in class now? *(Student A's book is open.)*
STUDENT B: Yes, I am. *(Student B's book is closed.)*

Example: at the library \ last night
STUDENT A: (. . .), were you at the library last night?
STUDENT B: No, I wasn't.
STUDENT A: Where were you?
STUDENT B: I was (at home / in my room / at a party, etc.)

1. at home \ now
2. at home \ yesterday morning
3. at home \ last night
4. in class \ two days ago
5. in *(name of a place in this city)* \ now
6. in *(name of this city)* \ last year
7. *(name of your teacher)* \ in class \ yesterday
8. *(names of two classmates)* \ here \ yesterday

Change roles. Student B should now ask Student A questions.

9. in *(name of this country)* \ two weeks ago
10. in *(name of this country)* \ two years ago
11. in *(name of a city)* \ now
12. at *(name of a park in this city)* \ yesterday afternoon
13. at *(name of a famous place in this city)* \ this morning★
14. at *(name of a popular place where students like to go)* \ last night
15. *(name of the teacher)* \ at home \ last night
16. *(names of two students)* \ *(name of this building)* \ yesterday afternoon

---

★Student B: If you are asking this question in the morning, use a present verb. If it is now afternoon or evening, use a past verb.

SIMPLE PRESENT:	(a) I	**walk**	to school	**every day**.	*verb* + **-ed** = the simple past tense
SIMPLE PAST:	(b) I	**walked**	to school	**yesterday**.	
SIMPLE PRESENT:	(c) Ann	**walks**	to school	**every day**.	
SIMPLE PAST:	(d) Ann	**walked**	to school	**yesterday**.	

I
you
she
he   } + *walked (verb +* **-ed***)*
it
we
they

■ **EXERCISE 7:** Complete the sentences. Use the words in the list; use the SIMPLE PRESENT or the SIMPLE PAST.

ask	✔ rain	wait
cook	shave	walk
dream	smile	watch
erase	stay	work

1. It often _____*rains*_____ in the morning. It _____*rained*_____ yesterday.

2. I _____ to school every morning. I _____ to school yesterday morning.

3. Sue often _____ questions. She _____ a question in class yesterday.

4. I _____ a movie on television last night. I usually

   _____ TV in the evening because I want to improve my English.

5. Mike _____ his own dinner yesterday evening. He

   _____ his own dinner every evening.

6. I usually _____ home at night because I have to study. I

   _____ home last night.

7. I have a job at the library. I _____ at the library every evening. I

   _____ there yesterday evening.

8. When I am asleep, I often _____. I _____ about my family last night.★

_____

★The past of *dream* can be *dreamed* or *dreamt*.

9. Linda usually _____ for the bus at a bus stop in front of her

   apartment building. She _____ for the bus there yesterday
   morning.

10. The teacher _____ some words from the board a couple of
    minutes ago. He used his hand instead of an eraser.

11. Our teacher is a warm, friendly person. She often _____ when
    she is talking to us.

12. Rick doesn't have a beard anymore. He _____ five days ago.

    Now he _____ every morning.

5-5 PAST TIME WORDS: *YESTERDAY, LAST,* AND *AGO*

NOTICE:
In (a): *yesterday* is used with *morning, afternoon,* and *evening.*
In (b): *last* is used with *night,* with long periods of time *(week, month, year),* with seasons *(spring, summer, etc.),* and with days of the week.
In (c): *ago* means "in the past." It follows specific lengths of time (e.g., *two minutes + ago, five years + ago*).

YESTERDAY	*LAST*	*AGO*

(a) Bob was here . . .
     yesterday.
     yesterday morning.
     yesterday afternoon.
     yesterday evening.
	(b) Sue was here . . .
	     last night.
	     last week.
	     last month.
	     last year.
	
	     last spring.
	     last summer.
	     last fall.
	     last winter.
	
	     last Monday.
	     last Tuesday.
	     last Wednesday.
	     etc.
		(c) Tom was here . . .
		     five minutes ago.
		     two hours ago.
		     three days ago.
		     a (one) week ago.
		     six months ago.
		     a (one) year ago.

■ **EXERCISE 8:** Use *yesterday* or *last*.

1. I dreamed about you _____*last*_____ night.

2. I was downtown _____ morning.

3. Two students were absent _____ Friday.

4. Ann wasn't at home _____ night.

5. Ann wasn't at home _____ evening.

6. Carmen was out of town _____ week.

7. I visited my aunt and uncle _____ fall.

8. Roberto walked home _____ afternoon.

9. My sister arrived in Miami _____ Sunday.

10. We watched TV _____ night.

11. Ali played with his children _____ evening.

12. Yoko arrived in Los Angeles _____ summer.

13. I visited my relatives in San Francisco _____ month.

14. My wife and I moved into a new house _____ year.

15. Mrs. Porter washed the kitchen floor _____ morning.

■ **EXERCISE 9:** Complete the sentences. Use *ago* in your completion.

1. I'm in class now, but I was at home _____*ten minutes ago/two hours ago/etc.*_____

2. I'm in class today, but I was absent from class _____

3. I'm in this country now, but I was in my country _____

4. I was in *(name of a city)* _____

5. I was in elementary school _____

6. I arrived in this city _____

7. There is a nice park in this city. I was at the park _____

8. We finished EXERCISE 2 _____

9. I was home in bed _____

10. It rained in this city _____

5-6 PRONUNCIATION OF -ED: /t/, /d/, AND /əd/

Final **-ed** has three pronunciations: /t/, /d/, and /əd/.

END OF VERB	SIMPLE FORM	SIMPLE PAST	PRONUNCIATION	
VOICELESS★	(a) *help* *laugh* *guess*	*helped* → *laughed* → *guessed* →	*help*/t/ *laugh*/t/ *guess*/t/★★	• Final **-ed** is pronounced /t/ if a verb ends in a voiceless sound, as in (a).
VOICED★	(b) *rub* *live* *seem*	*rubbed* → *lived* → *seemed* →	*rub*/d/ *liv*/d/ *seem*/d/	• Final **-ed** is pronounced /d/ if the simple form of the verb ends in a voiced sound, as in (b).
-*d* or -*t*	(c) *need* *want*	*needed* → *wanted* →	*need*/əd/ *want*/əd/	• Final **-ed** is pronounced /əd/ if a verb ends in the letters "d" or "t," as in (c).

★ See Chart 2-4 for information about voiced and voiceless sounds.
★★ The words *guessed* and *guest* have the same pronunciation.

■ **EXERCISE 10:** Read the words aloud. Then use the words to complete the sentences.

GROUP A: Final **-ed** is pronounced /t/ after voiceless sounds:

1. walked	✔ 5. watched	9. kissed	13. laughed
2. worked	6. touched	10. erased	14. coughed
3. cooked	7. washed	11. helped	
4. asked	8. finished	12. stopped	

15. I _____ *watched* _____ TV last night.

16. Anna _____ to class yesterday instead of taking the bus.

17. I _____ the dirty dishes after dinner last night.

18. Jim _____ the board with an eraser.

19. Robert loves his daughter. He _____ her on the forehead.

20. The joke was funny. We _____ at the funny story.

21. The rain _____ a few minutes ago. The sky is clear now.

22. I worked for three hours last night. I _____ my homework about nine o'clock.

23. Steve _____ my shoulder with his hand to get my attention.

24. Mr. Wilson _____ in his garden yesterday morning.

25. Judy _____ because she was sick. She had the flu.

26. Don is a good cook. He _____ some delicious food last night.

27. Linda _____ a question in class yesterday.

28. I had a problem with my homework. The teacher _____ me before class.

GROUP B: Final *-ed* is pronounced /d/ after voiced sounds:

1. rained	5. smiled	9. remembered
2. signed	6. killed	10. played
3. shaved	7. sneezed	11. enjoyed
4. arrived	8. closed	12. snowed

13. It's winter. The ground is white because it _____ yesterday.

14. Anita _____ in this city three weeks ago. She

_____ at the airport on September 3rd.★

15. The girls and boys _____ baseball after school yesterday.

16. When Ali got a new credit card, he _____ his name in ink on the back of the card.

17. Rick used to have a beard, but now he doesn't. He _____ this morning.

18. The students' test papers were very good. The teacher, Mr. Jackson, was very

pleased. He _____ when he returned the test papers.

19. I _____ the party last night. It was fun. I had a good time.

20. The window was open. Mr. Chan _____ it because it was cold outside.

21. The streets were wet this morning because it _____ last night.

22. "Achoo!" When Judy _____, Ken said, "Bless you." Oscar said, "Gesundheit!"

★Notice preposition usage after *arrive*:

    I arrive *in* a country or *in* a city.

    I arrive *at* a particular place (a building, an airport, a house, an apartment, a party, etc.)

Arrive is followed by either *in* or *at*. **Arrive** is not followed by *to*.

    INCORRECT: *She arrived to the United States.*

    INCORRECT: *She arrived to the airport.*

23. I have my books with me. I didn't forget them today. I

_____ to bring them to class.

24. Mrs. Lane was going crazy because there was a fly in the room. The fly was buzzing all around

the room. Finally, she _____
it with a rolled up newspaper.

GROUP C: Final **-ed** is pronounced /əd/ after /t/ and /d/:

1. waited	5. invited
2. wanted	6. needed
3. counted	7. added
4. visited	8. folded

9. The children _____ some candy after dinner.

10. Mr. Miller _____ to stay in the hospital for two weeks after he had an operation.

11. I _____ the number of students in the room.

12. Mr. and Mrs. Johnson _____ us to come to their house last Sunday.

13. Last Sunday we _____ the Johnsons.

14. I _____ the letter before I put it in the envelope.

15. Kim _____ for the bus at the corner of 5th Avenue and Main Street.

16. The boy _____ the numbers on the chalkboard in arithmetic class yesterday.

■ **EXERCISE 11—ORAL (BOOKS CLOSED):**   Practice pronouncing -*ed*.

Example: walk to the front of the room
STUDENT A: *(Student A walks to the front of the room.)*
TEACHER: What did (. . .) do?
STUDENT B: She/He walked to the front of the room.
TEACHER: What did you do?
STUDENT A: I walked to the front of the room.

1. smile	11. wash your hands *(pantomime)*
2. laugh	12. touch the floor
3. cough	13. point at the door
4. sneeze	14. fold a piece of paper
5. shave *(pantomime)*	15. count your fingers
6. erase the board	16. push *(something in the room)*
7. sign your name	17. pull *(something in the room)*
8. open the door	18. yawn
9. close the door	19. pick up your pen
10. ask a question	20. add two and two on the board

5-7   SPELLING OF -*ED* VERBS

		END OF VERB	→	-*ED* FORM
Rule 1:		END OF VERB: A CONSONANT + -*e* smi*le* era*se*	→	ADD -*d* smi*led* era*sed*
Rule 2:		ONE VOWEL + ONE CONSONANT★ st*op* r*ub*	→	DOUBLE THE CONSONANT, ADD -*ed* st*opped* r*ubbed*
Rule 3:		TWO VOWELS + ONE CONSONANT r*ain* n*eed*	→	ADD -*ed*; DO NOT DOUBLE THE CONSONANT r*ained* n*eeded*
Rule 4:		TWO CONSONANTS cou*nt* he*lp*	→	ADD -*ed*; DO NOT DOUBLE THE CONSONANT cou*nted* he*lped*
Rule 5:		CONSONANT + -*y* stu*dy* car*ry*	→	CHANGE -*y* TO -*i*, ADD -*ed* stu*died* car*ried*
Rule 6:		VOWEL + -*y* pl*ay* enj*oy*	→	ADD -*ed*; DO NOT CHANGE -*y* TO -*i* pl*ayed* enj*oyed*

★EXCEPTIONS: Do not double *x* (*fix* + -*ed* = *fixed*). Do not double *w* (*snow* + -*ed* = *snowed*).
NOTE: For two-syllable verbs that end in a vowel and a consonant (e.g., *visit, open*), see Chart 5-8.

■ **EXERCISE 12:** Give the *-ed* and *-ing* forms of these words.★

		-ED	-ING
1.	count	*counted*	*counting*
2.	stop		
3.	smile		
4.	rain		
5.	help		
6.	dream		
7.	clap		
8.	erase		
9.	rub		
10.	yawn		
11.	study		
12.	stay		
13.	worry		
14.	enjoy		

■ **EXERCISE 13:** Use the correct form of the words in the list to complete the sentences.

carry	✔ finish	stay
clap	learn	stop
cry	rub	taste
enjoy	smile	wait
fail		

1. I _____*finished*_____ my homework at nine last night.

2. We _____ some new vocabulary yesterday.

3. I _____ the soup before dinner last night. It was delicious.

4. Linda _____ for the bus at the corner yesterday.

5. The bus _____ at the corner. It was on time.

_____
★See Chart 5-8 for the spelling of *-ing* forms.

6. We _____ the play at the theater last night. It was very good.

7. At the theater last night, the audience _____ when the play was over.

8. Ann _____ her suitcases to the bus station yesterday. They weren't heavy.

9. The baby _____ her eyes because she was sleepy.

10. I _____ home and watched a sad movie on TV last night. I

    _____ at the end of the movie.

11. Mike _____ his examination last week. His grade was "F."

12. Jane _____ at the children. She was happy to see them.

■ **EXERCISE 14:** Write the correct spelling of the **-ed** form. Then write the correct pronunciation of the **-ed** form: /t/, /d/, or /əd/.

	-ED FORM		PRONUNCIATION
1. wait	waited	wait +	/əd/
2. spell	spelled	spell +	/d/
3. kiss	kissed	kiss +	/t/
4. plan	_____	plan +	_____
5. join	_____	join +	_____
6. hope	_____	hope +	_____
7. drop	_____	drop +	_____
8. add	_____	add +	_____
9. point	_____	point +	_____
10. pat	_____	pat +	_____
11. shout	_____	shout +	_____
12. reply	_____	reply +	_____
13. play	_____	play +	_____
14. touch	_____	touch +	_____
15. end	_____	end +	_____

You may not know the meanings of the following words. Figure out the spelling and pronunciation of the **-ed** forms even if you don't know the meanings of the words.

16. mop	_____	mop	+	_____
17. droop	_____	droop	+	_____
18. cope	_____	cope	+	_____
19. rant	_____	rant	+	_____
20. date	_____	date	+	_____
21. heat	_____	heat	+	_____
22. bat	_____	bat	+	_____
23. trick	_____	trick	+	_____
24. fool	_____	fool	+	_____
25. reward	_____	reward	+	_____
26. grab	_____	grab	+	_____
27. dance	_____	dance	+	_____
28. paste	_____	paste	+	_____
29. earn	_____	earn	+	_____
30. grin	_____	grin	+	_____
31. mend	_____	mend	+	_____

5-8 SPELLING OF -ED AND -ING: TWO-SYLLABLE VERBS

	VERB	SPEAKING STRESS		
(a)	visit	VIS · it		
(b)	admit	ad · MIT		

Some verbs have two syllables. In (a): *visit* has two syllables: *vis + it*. In the word *visit*, the stress is on the first syllable. In (b): the stress is on the second syllable in the word *admit*.

	VERB	STRESS	-ED FORM	-ING FORM
(c)	visit	VIS · it	visited	visiting
(d)	open	O · pen	opened	opening
(e)	admit	ad · MIT	admitted	admitting
(f)	occur	oc · CUR	occurred	occurring

For two-syllable verbs that end in a vowel and a consonant:
- The consonant is not doubled if the stress is on the first syllable, as in (c) and (d).
- The consonant is doubled if the stress is on the second syllable, as in (e) and (f).

■ **EXERCISE 15:** Write the *-ed* and *-ing* forms of the given VERBS.

	VERB	STRESS	-ED FORM	-ING FORM
1.	answer	**AN** · swer★	*answered*	*answering*
2.	prefer	pre · **FER**		
3.	happen	**HAP** · pen		
4.	visit	**VIS** · it		
5.	permit	per · **MIT**		
6.	listen	**LIS** · ten★★		
7.	offer	**OF** · fer		
8.	occur	oc · **CUR**		
9.	open	**O** · pen		
10.	enter	**EN** · ter		
11.	refer	re · **FER**		
12.	begin	be · **GIN**	*(none)*★★★	

■ **EXERCISE 16:** Complete the sentences with the VERBS in the list. Use the *-ed* forms. Use each verb only one time.

admit	*listen*	*open*
✔ *answer*	*occur*	*permit*
happen	*offer*	*visit*

1. The teacher _____*answered*_____ a question for me in class.

2. Yesterday I _____ my aunt and uncle at their home.

3. We _____ to some music after dinner last night.

4. It was okay for the children to have some candy after lunch. Mrs. King

    _____ them to have a little candy.

5. I _____ the window because the room was hot.

★ The "w" is not pronounced in *answer*.
★★ The "t" is not pronounced in *listen*.
★★★ The verb *begin* does not have an *-ed* form. Its past form is irregular: *began*.

6. A car accident _____ at the corner of 5th Street and Main yesterday.

7. A bicycle accident _____ on Forest Avenue yesterday.

8. My friend poured a glass of water and held it toward me. She asked me if I wanted it.

   She _____ me a glass of water.

9. A man unlocked the gate and _____ the sports fans into the stadium.

■ **EXERCISE 17—ORAL/WRITTEN (BOOKS CLOSED):** This is a spelling test. Give the *-ed* form of each word.

1. stop	6. rain	11. carry	16. occur
2. wait	7. permit	12. open	17. stay
3. study	8. listen	13. fold	18. help
4. smile	9. rub	14. offer	19. drop
5. enjoy	10. visit	15. happen	20. count

■ **EXERCISE 18:** Complete the sentences. Use the words in parentheses. Use the SIMPLE PRESENT, PRESENT PROGRESSIVE, or SIMPLE PAST. Pay attention to spelling and pronunciation.

1. I (walk) _____ *walked* _____ to school yesterday.

2. I (sit) _____ *am sitting* _____ in class right now.

3. I usually (go) _____ *go* _____ to bed at eleven o'clock every night.

4. Sally (finish) _____ her homework at ten o'clock last night.

5. I *(study)* _____ at the library yesterday.

6. I *(study)* _____ English every day.

7. I am in class right now. I *(study)* _____ English.

8. I need an umbrella because it *(rain)* _____ right now.

9. It *(rain)* _____ yesterday morning.

10. My roommate *(help)* _____ me with my homework last night.

11. We can go outside now. The rain *(stop)* _____ a few
minutes ago.

12. The children are in the park. They *(play)* _____ baseball.

13. I *(play)* _____ soccer last week.

14. Yesterday morning I *(brush)* _____ my teeth, *(wash)*

_____ my face, and *(shave)* _____.

15. Ann is in her living room right now. She *(watch)* _____
television.

16. Ann usually *(watch)* _____ TV in the evening.

17. She *(watch)* _____ a good program on TV last night.

18. We *(do)* _____ an exercise in class right now. We *(use)*

_____ verb tenses in sentences.

19. I *(arrive)* _____ in this city a month ago.

20. Matt *(listen)* _____ to music every morning while he's
getting ready to go to school.

21. A: Where's Matt?
    B: He's in his room?

    A: What *(do, he)* _____?

    B: He *(listen)* _____ to music.

22. A: *(you, listen)* _____ to the news every day?

    B: Yes. I *(like)* _____ to know about events in the world.

    I usually *(listen)* _____ to the news on TV before I go

    to sleep at night, but last night I *(listen)* _____ to the
    news on the radio.

5-9 THE SIMPLE PAST: IRREGULAR VERBS

Some verbs do not have **-ed** forms. The past form is irregular.

PRESENT	PAST	
come	– came	(a) I **come** to class **every day**.
do	– did	(b) I *came* to class **yesterday**.
eat	– ate	
get	– got	(c) I **do** my homework **every day**.
go	– went	(d) I *did* my homework **yesterday**.
have	– had	
put	– put	(e) Ann **eats** breakfast **every morning**.
see	– saw	(f) Ann *ate* breakfast **yesterday morning**.
sit	– sat	
sleep	– slept	
stand	– stood	
write	– wrote	

■ **EXERCISE 19—ORAL:**   Change the sentences to the past.

1. Tom gets some mail every day.
   → *Tom got some mail yesterday.*
2. They go downtown every day.
3. We have lunch every day.
4. I see my friends every day.
5. Hamid sits in the front row every day.
6. I sleep for eight hours every night.
7. The students stand in line at the cafeteria.
8. I write a letter to my parents every week.
9. Wai-Leng comes to class late every day.
10. We do exercises in class every day.
11. I eat breakfast every morning.
12. I get up at seven every day.
13. Robert puts his books in his briefcase every day.

■ **EXERCISE 20—ORAL (BOOKS CLOSED):**   Change the sentences to the past.

Example: I come to class every day.
Response: I came to class yesterday.

1. I eat lunch every day.
2. I see you every day.
3. I sit in class every day.
4. I write a letter every day.
5. I do my homework every day.
6. I have breakfast every day.
7. I go downtown every day.
8. I get up at eight every day.
9. I stand at the bus stop every day.
10. I sleep for eight hours every night.
11. I come to school every day.
12. I put my pen in my pocket every day.

■ **EXERCISE 21:** Complete the sentences. Use the words in parentheses. Use SIMPLE PRESENT, PRESENT PROGRESSIVE, or SIMPLE PAST. Pay attention to spelling and pronunciation.

1. I *(get)* _____got_____ up at eight o'clock yesterday morning.

2. Mary *(talk)* _____ to John on the phone last night.

3. Mary *(talk)* _____ to John on the phone right now.

4. Mary *(talk)* _____ to John on the phone every day.

5. Jim and I *(eat)* _____ lunch at the cafeteria two hours ago.

6. We *(eat)* _____ lunch at the cafeteria every day.

7. I *(go)* _____ to bed early last night.

8. My roommate *(study)* _____ Spanish last year.

9. Sue *(write)* _____ a letter to her parents yesterday.

10. Sue *(write)* _____ a letter to her parents every week.

11. Sue is in her room right now. She *(sit)* _____ at her desk.

12. Maria *(do)* _____ her homework last night.

13. Yesterday I *(see)* _____ Fumiko at the library.

14. I *(have)* _____ a dream last night. I *(dream)* _____
    about my friends. I *(sleep)* _____ for eight hours.

15. A strange thing *(happen)* _____ to me yesterday. I couldn't
    remember my own telephone number.

16. My wife *(come)* _____ home around five every day.

17. Yesterday she *(come)* _____ home at 5:15.

18. Our teacher *(stand)* _____ in the middle of the room right now.

19. Our teacher *(stand)* _____ in the front of the room yesterday.

20. Tom *(put)* _____ the butter in the refrigerator yesterday.

21. He *(put)* _____ the milk in the refrigerator every day.

22. Pablo usually *(sit)* _____ in the back of the room, but yesterday

    he *(sit)* _____ in the front row. Today he *(be)* _____

    absent. He *(be)* _____ absent two days ago too.

SUBJECT	+	DID	+	NOT	+	MAIN VERB		
(a)	I	**did**		**not**		**walk**	to school yesterday.	
(b)	You	**did**		**not**		**walk**	to school yesterday.	
(c)	Tom	**did**		**not**		**eat**	lunch yesterday.	
(d)	They	**did**		**not**		**come**	to class yesterday.	

$$\left.\begin{array}{l}I\\ you\\ she\\ he\\ it\\ we\\ they\end{array}\right\}$$ + **did not** + *main verb** (simple form)

(e) INCORRECT: I *did not walked* to school yesterday. (f) INCORRECT: Tom *did not ate* lunch yesterday.	Notice that the simple form of the main verb is used with **did not**.
(g) I **didn't walk** to school yesterday. (h) Tom **didn't eat** lunch yesterday.	Negative contraction: **did** + **not** = **didn't**

*EXCEPTION: **did** is NOT used when the main verb is **be**. See Charts 5-2 and 5-3.
INCORRECT: Joe *didn't be* here yesterday.
CORRECT: Joe *wasn't* here yesterday.

■ **EXERCISE 22— ORAL (BOOKS CLOSED):** Use "*I don't ... every day*" and "*I didn't ... yesterday.*"

Example: walk to school
Response: I don't walk to school every day. I didn't walk to school yesterday.

1. eat breakfast	5. study	9. do my homework
2. watch TV	6. go to the library	10. shave
3. go shopping	7. visit my friends	
4. read the newspaper	8. see (. . .)	

■ **EXERCISE 23—ORAL (BOOKS CLOSED):** Practice present and past negatives.

STUDENT A: Use **I don't** and **I didn't**. Use an appropriate past time expression with **didn't.**

STUDENT B: Report what Student A said. Use **she/he doesn't** and then **she/he didn't** with an appropriate past time expression.

Example: walk to school every morning
STUDENT A: I don't walk to school every morning. I didn't walk to school yesterday morning.
TEACHER: Tell me about (Student A).
STUDENT B: She/He doesn't walk to school every morning. She/He didn't walk to school yesterday morning.

1. eat breakfast every morning	6. dream in English every night
2. watch TV every night	7. visit my aunt and uncle every year
3. talk to (. . .) every day	8. write to my parents every week
4. play soccer every afternoon	9. read the newspaper every morning
5. study grammar every evening	10. pay all of my bills every month

■ **EXERCISE 24:** Complete the sentences. Use the words in parentheses. Use SIMPLE PRESENT, SIMPLE PAST, or PRESENT PROGRESSIVE.

1. I (go, not) _____*didn't go*_____ to a movie last night. I (stay)

   _____*stayed*_____ home.

2. Mike (come, not) _____*doesn't come*_____ to class every day.

3. I (finish, not) _____ my homework last night. I (go)

   _____ to bed early.

4. Jane (stand, not) _____ up right now. She (sit)

   _____ down.

5. It (rain, not) _____ right now. The rain (stop)

   _____ a few minutes ago.

6. The weather (be, not) _____ cold today, but it (be) _____
   cold yesterday.

7. Tina and I (go, not) _____ shopping yesterday. We (go)

   _____ shopping last Monday.

8. I (go) _____ to a movie last night, but I (enjoy, not) _____

   it. It (be, not) _____ very good.

9. I (write) _____ a letter to my girlfriend yesterday, but I (write, not)

   _____ a letter to her last week.

10. Sue (read) _____ a magazine right now. She (watch, not)

    _____ TV.

11. My husband *(come, not)* _____ home for dinner last night.

12. The children *(go)* _____ to bed a half an hour ago. They *(sleep)*

_____ now.

13. We *(be)* _____ late for the movie last night. The movie *(start)*

_____ at seven, but we *(arrive, not)* _____

until seven-fifteen.

14. Olga *(ask)* _____ Hamid a question a few minutes ago, but he

(answer, not) _____ her question.

15. Toshi is a busy student. He usually *(eat, not)* _____

lunch because he *(have, not)* _____ enough time
between classes.

16. He *(eat)* _____ lunch the day before yesterday, but he *(eat, not)*

_____ lunch yesterday.

5-11 THE SIMPLE PAST: *YES/NO* QUESTIONS

DID + SUBJECT + MAIN VERB			SHORT ANSWER + (LONG ANSWER)	
(a) **Did**	*Mary*	*walk* to school? → →	**Yes, she did**. **No, she didn't**.	(She walked to school.) (She didn't walk to school.)
(b) **Did**	*you*	*come* to class? → →	**Yes, I did**. **No, I didn't**.	(I came to class.) (I didn't come to class.)

■ **EXERCISE 25:** Make questions. Give short answers.

1. A: *Did you walk downtown yesterday?* _____

   B: *Yes, I did.* _____ (I walked downtown yesterday.)

2. A: *Did it rain last week?* _____

   B: *No, it didn't.* _____ (It didn't rain last week.)

3. A: _____

   B: _____ (I ate lunch at the cafeteria.)

4. A: _____

   B: _____ (Mr. Kwan didn't go out of town last week.)

5. A: _____

   B: _____ (I had a cup of tea this morning.)

6. A: _____

   B: _____ (Benito and I went to a party last night.)

7. A: _____

   B: _____ (Olga studied English in high school.)

8. A: _____

   B: _____ (Yoko and Ali didn't do their homework last night.)

9. A: _____

   B: _____ (I saw Gina at dinner last night.)

10. A: _____

    B: _____ (I didn't dream in English last night.)

■ **EXERCISE 26:** Complete the sentences with *was*, *were*, or *did*.

1. I _____*did*_____ not go to work yesterday. I _____*was*_____ sick, so I stayed home
   from the office.

2. Tom _____ not in his office yesterday. He _____ not go to work.

3. A: _____ Mr. Chan in his office yesterday?
   B: Yes.

   A: _____ you see him about your problem?

   B: Yes. He answered all my questions. He _____ very helpful.

4. A: _____ you at the meeting yesterday?
   B: What meeting?

   A: _____ you forget about the meeting?
   B: I guess so. What meeting?
   A: The meeting with the president of the company about employee benefits.

   B: Oh. Now I remember. No, I _____ not there. _____ you?
   A: Yes. I can tell you all about it.
   B: Thanks.

5. A: Where _____ you yesterday?

   B: I _____ at the zoo.

   A: _____ you enjoy it?

   B: Yes, but the weather _____ very hot. I tried to stay out of the sun. Most

   of the animals _____ in their houses or in the shade. The sun

   _____ too hot for them, too. They _____ not want to be
   outside in the hot sun.

■ **EXERCISE 27:** Make questions. Give short answers.

   1. A: _____*Were you at home last night?*_____

      B: _____*No, I wasn't.*_____ (I wasn't at home last night.)

      A: _____*Did you go to a movie?*_____

      B: _____*Yes, I did.*_____ (I went to a movie.)

   2. A: _____

      B: _____ (It isn't cold today.)

   3. A: _____

      B: _____ (I come to class every day.)

   4. A: _____

      B : _____ (Roberto was absent yesterday.)

   5. A: _____

      B: _____ (Roberto stayed home yesterday.)

   6. A: _____

      B: _____ (I don't watch television every day.)

   7. A: _____

      B: _____ (Mohammed isn't in class today.)

      A: _____

      B: _____ (He was here yesterday.)

      A: _____

      B: _____ (He came to class the day before yesterday.)

      A: _____

      B: _____ (He usually comes to class every day.)

8. A: _____

   B: _____ (I live in an apartment.)

   A: _____

   B: _____ (I don't have a roommate.)

   A: _____

   B: _____ (I don't want a roommate.)

   A: _____

   B: _____ (I had a roommate last year.) It didn't work out.

   A: _____

   B: _____ (He was difficult to live with.)
   A: What did he do?
   B: He never picked up his dirty clothes. He never washed his dirty dishes. He was always late with his share of the rent.

   A: _____

   B: _____ (I asked him to keep the apartment clean.) He always agreed, but he never did it.

   A: _____

   B: _____ (I was glad when he left.) I like living alone.

■ **EXERCISE 28—ORAL (BOOKS CLOSED):**   Ask a classmate a question about her/his activities this morning.

   Example: walk to school
   STUDENT A: Did you walk to school this morning?
   STUDENT B: Yes, I did. OR: No, I didn't.

   1. get up at seven
   2. eat breakfast
   3. study English
   4. walk to class
   5. talk to (. . .)
   6. see (. . .)
   7. smoke a cigarette
   8. go shopping
   9. have a cup of coffee
   10. watch TV
   11. listen to the radio
   12. read a newspaper

■ **EXERCISE 29—ORAL (BOOKS CLOSED):** Ask questions about the present and the past.

Example: walk to school
STUDENT A: Do you walk to school every day?
STUDENT B: Yes, I do. OR: No, I don't.
STUDENT A: Did you walk to school this morning?
STUDENT B: Yes, I did. OR: No, I didn't.

1. go downtown
2. dream in color
3. talk to (. . .) on the phone
4. come to (grammar) class
5. sing in the shower
6. eat at least two pieces of fresh fruit
7. think about your family
8. cook your own dinner

9. wear *(an article of clothing)*
10. laugh out loud at least two times
11. speak *(name of a language)*
12. go to *(name of a place in this city)*
13. read at least one book
14. go swimming
15. go shopping

■ **EXERCISE 30—ORAL (BOOKS CLOSED):** Review of irregular verbs. Answer all the questions "yes." Give both a short answer and a long answer.

Example: Did you come to class today?
Response: Yes, I did. I came to class today.

1. Did you eat dinner last night?
2. Did (. . .) come to class today?
3. Did you get a letter yesterday?
4. Did (. . .) go shopping yesterday?
5. Did (. . .) do his/her homework last night?
6. Did you sleep well last night?
7. Did you have a cup of coffee this morning?
8. Did (. . .) go to a movie last night?
9. Did (. . .) sit in that chair yesterday?
10. Did you write a letter yesterday.?
11. *(Tell a student to stand up.)* Did (. . .) stand up? *(Tell him/her to sit down.)* Did (. . .) sit down?
12. Did (. . .) put his/her books on his/her desk this *(morning | afternoon | evening)?*

5-12 MORE IRREGULAR VERBS

bring - brought	*drive - drove*	*run - ran*
buy - bought	*read - read★*	*teach - taught*
catch - caught	*ride - rode*	*think - thought*
drink - drank		

★The past form of *read* is pronounced the same as the color red.

■ **EXERCISE 31—ORAL (BOOKS CLOSED):** Practice using irregular verbs.

Example: teach-taught
TEACHER: teach, taught. I teach class every day. I taught class yesterday. What did I do yesterday?
STUDENTS: teach, taught. You taught class.

1. *bring-brought*   I bring my book to class every day. I brought my book to class yesterday. What did I do yesterday?

2. *buy-bought*   I buy books at the bookstore. I bought a book yesterday. What did I do yesterday?

3. *teach-taught*   I teach class every day. I taught class yesterday. What did I do yesterday?

4. *catch-caught*   I catch the bus every day. I caught the bus yesterday. What did I do yesterday?

5. *think-thought*   I often think about my family. I thought about my family yesterday. What did I do yesterday?

6. REVIEW: What did I bring to class yesterday? What did you bring yesterday?

    What did I buy yesterday? What did you buy yesterday?

    Did you teach class yesterday? Who did?

    Did I walk to class yesterday or did I catch the bus?

    What did I think about yesterday? What did you think about yesterday?

7. *run-ran*   Sometimes I'm late for class, so I run. Yesterday I was late, so I ran. What did I do yesterday?

8. *read-read*   I like to read books. I read every day. Yesterday I read a book. What did I do yesterday? What did you read yesterday?

9. *drink-drank*   I usually drink a cup of coffee in the morning. I drank a cup of coffee this morning. What did I do this morning? Did you drink a cup of coffee this morning?

10. *drive-drove*   I usually drive my car to school. I drove my car to school this morning. What did I do this morning? Who has a car? Did you drive to school this morning?

11. *ride-rode*   Sometimes I ride the bus to school. I rode the bus yesterday morning. What did I do yesterday morning? Who rode the bus to school this morning?

12. REVIEW: I was late for class yesterday morning, so what did I do?

    What did I read yesterday? What did you read yesterday?

    Did you read a newspaper this morning?

    What did I drink this morning? What did you drink this morning?

    I have a car. Did I drive to school this morning? Did you?

    Did you ride the bus to school this morning?

■ **EXERCISE 32:** Complete the sentences. Use the words in parentheses.

1. A: Why are you out of breath?

   B: I *(run)* _____ to class because I was late.

2. A: *(Ms. Carter, teach)* _____ class
   yesterday?

   B: No, she didn't. Mr. Adams *(teach)* _____ our class.

3. A: I *(ride)* _____ the bus to school yesterday. How did you
   get to school?

   B: I *(drive)* _____ my car.

4. A: Did you decide to change schools?

   B: I *(think)* _____ about it, but then I decided to stay here.

5. A: *(you, go)* _____ shopping yesterday?

   B: Yes. I *(buy)* _____ a new pair of shoes.

6. A: *(you, study)* _____ last night?

   B: No, I didn't. I was tired. I *(read)* _____ a magazine and then

   (go) _____ to bed early.

7. A: Do you like milk?

   B: No. I *(drink)* _____ milk when I *(be)* _____ a child,
   but I don't like milk now.

8. A: Did you leave your dictionary at home?

   B: No. I *(bring)* _____ it to class with me.

9. A: Did you enjoy your fishing trip?

   B: I had a wonderful time! I *(catch)* _____ a lot of fish.

■ **EXERCISE 33:** Complete the sentences. Use the verbs in parentheses.

1. Ann and I *(go)* _____ to the bookstore yesterday. I *(buy)*

   _____ some stationery and a T-shirt.

2. I had to go downtown yesterday. I *(catch)* _____ the bus in front

   of my apartment and *(ride)* _____ to Grand Avenue. Then I

   (get off) _____ the bus and transferred to another one. It *(be)*

   _____ a long trip.

3. Sue *(eat)* _____ popcorn and *(drink)* _____ a

   cola at the movie theater last night. I *(eat, not)* _____ anything.
   I'm on a diet.

4. Maria *(ask)* _____ the teacher a question in class yesterday. The

   teacher *(think)* _____ about the question for a few minutes and
   then said, "I don't know."

5. I *(want)* _____ *(go)* _____ to the basketball

   game last night, but I *(stay)* _____ home because I had to study.

6. Last night I *(read)* _____ an article in the newspaper. It *(be)*

   _____ about the snowstorm in Moscow.

7. Yesterday Yoko *(teach)* _____ us how to say "thank you" in

   Japanese. Kim *(teach)* _____ us how to say "I love you" in
   Korean.

8. When Ben and I *(go)* ____ _____ to the department store yesterday, I

   (buy) _____ some new socks. Ben *(buy, not)* _____ anything.

9. Rita *(pass, not)* _____ the test yesterday. She *(fail)*

   _____ it.

10. Last summer we *(drive)* _____ to Colorado for our vacation. We

    (visit) _____ a national park, where we *(camp)* _____

    in our tent for a week. We *(go)* _____ fishing one morning. I

    (catch) _____ a

    very big fish, but my husband

    (catch, not) _____

    anything. We *(enjoy)* _____

    cooking and eating the fish for dinner.

    It *(be)* _____ delicious.

    I like fresh fish.

11. I almost *(have)* _____ an accident yesterday. A dog *(run)*

_____ into the street in front of my car. I *(slam)*

_____ on my brakes and just *(miss)* _____ the dog.

12. Yesterday I *(play)* _____ ball with my little boy. He *(catch)*

_____ the ball most of the time, but sometimes he *(drop)*

_____ it.

■ **EXERCISE 34—ORAL (BOOKS CLOSED):** Ask and answer questions using the SIMPLE
PAST.
STUDENT A: Ask a classmate a question. Use the given verb. Use the past tense.
STUDENT B: Answer the question. Give both a short answer and a long answer.

Example: drink
STUDENT A: Did you drink a cup of coffee this morning?
STUDENT B: Yes, I did. I drank a cup of coffee this morning. OR: No, I didn't. I didn't
drink a cup of coffee this morning.

1. eat	7. drink	13. walk
2. buy	8. read	14. watch
3. get up	9. drive	15. listen to
4. have	10. sleep	16. see
5. go	11. go	17. think about
6. study	12. talk to	18. rain

■ **EXERCISE 35—WRITTEN:** Use the expressions in the list below to write sentences about
yourself. When did you do these things *in the past?* Use the SIMPLE PAST tense and
past time expressions *(yesterday, two days ago, last week, etc.)* in all of your sentences.

Example: go downtown with *(someone)*
Response: I went downtown with Marco two days ago.

1. arrive in *(this city)*	12. talk to *(someone)* on the phone
2. write a letter to *(someone)*	13. go shopping
3. eat at a restaurant	14. study English
4. go to bed early	15. read a newspaper
5. buy *(something)*	16. go on a picnic
6. go to bed late	17. go to a party
7. get up early	18. play *(soccer, a pinball machine, etc.)*
8. be late for class	19. see *(someone or something)*
9. have a cold	20. think about *(someone or something)*
10. be in elementary school	21. do my homework
11. drink a cup of tea	22. be born

5-13 THE SIMPLE PAST: USING *WHERE, WHEN, WHAT TIME,* AND *WHY*

QUESTION							SHORT ANSWER
(a)		*Did*	you	*go*	downtown?	→	Yes, I did. / No, I didn't.
(b)	***Where***	*did*	you	*go?*		→	***Downtown***.
(c)		*Did*	you	*run*	because you were late?	→	Yes, I did. / No, I didn't.
(d)	***Why***	*did*	you	*run?*		→	***Because I was late***.
(e)		*Did*	Ann	*come*	at six?	→	Yes, she did. / No, she didn't.
(f)	***When*** ⎱ ***What time*** ⎰	*did*	Ann	*come?*		→	***At six***.

COMPARE:	
(g) ***What time*** did Ann come? → ***At six***. → ***Seven o'clock***. → ***Around 9:30***.	***What time*** usually asks specifically for time on a clock.
(h) ***When*** did Ann come? → ***At six***. → ***Friday***. → ***June 15th***. → ***Last week***. → ***Three days ago***.	The answer to ***when*** can be various expressions of time.

■ **EXERCISE 36:** Make questions. Use ***where, when, what time,*** or ***why.***

1. A: ___*Where did you go yesterday?*___
   B: To the zoo. (I went to the zoo yesterday.)

2. A: _____
   B: Last month. (Jason arrived in Canada last month.)

3. A: _____
   B: At 7:05. (My plane arrived at 7:05.)

4. A: _____
   B: Because I was tired. (I stayed home last night because I was tired.)

5. A: _____
   B: At the library. (I studied at the library last night.)

6. A: _____
   B: Because it's dark in here. (I turned on the light because it's dark in here.)

7. A: _____
   B: To Greece. (Sara went to Greece for her vacation.)

8. A: _____
   B: Around midnight. (I finished my homework around midnight.)

9. A: _____
   B: Five weeks ago. (I came to this city five weeks ago.)

10. A: _____
    B: Because Tony made a funny face. (I laughed because Tony made a funny face.)

11. A: _____
    B: At Emerhoff's Shoe Store. (I got my sandals at Emerhoff's Shoe Store.)

12. A: _____
    B: Upstairs. (Kate is upstairs.)

13. A: _____
    B: In the dormitory. (Ben lives in the dormitory.)

14. A: _____
    B: To the park. (I went to the park yesterday afternoon.)

15. A: _____
    B: Because he's sick. (Bobby is in bed because he's sick.)

16. A: _____
    B: Because he was sick. (Bobby stayed home because he was sick.)

17. A: _____
    B: 7:20. (The movie starts at 7:20.)

18. A: _____
    B: Two days ago. (Sara got back from Brazil two days ago.)

19. A: _____
    B: Because she wanted to talk to Joe. (Tina called because she wanted to talk to Joe.)

20. A: _____
    B: Because he wants big muscles. (Jim lifts weights because he wants big muscles.)

■ EXERCISE 37—ORAL (BOOKS CLOSED): Make questions. Use question words.

Example: I got up at 7:30.
Response: When/What time did you get up?

1. I went to the zoo.
2. I went to the zoo yesterday.
3. I went to the zoo yesterday because I wanted to see the animals.
4. (. . .) went to the park.
5. (. . .) went to the park yesterday.
6. (. . .) went to the park yesterday because the weather was nice.
7. I am in class.
8. I came to class (an hour) ago.
9. (. . .) is in class.
10. (. . .) came to class (an hour) ago.
11. (. . .) studied at the library last night.
12. (. . .) finished his/her homework around midnight.
13. (. . .) went to bed at 7:30 last night.
14. (. . .) went to bed early because he/she was tired.
15. (. . .) went to the park.
16. (. . .) went to the park yesterday.
17. (. . .) went to the park yesterday because he/she wanted to jog.
18. (. . .) is absent today because he/she is sick.
19. (. . .) is at home.
20. (. . .) stayed home because he/she is sick.

■ EXERCISE 38: Complete the dialogues with questions that begin with *why didn't*.

1. A: _____*Why didn't you come to class?*_____
   B: Because I was sick.

2. A: _____
   B: Because I didn't have enough time.

3. A: _____
   B: Because I forgot your phone number.

4. A: _____
   B: Because I had a headache.

5. A: _____
   B: Because I wasn't hungry.

6. A: _____
   B: Because I didn't want to.

■ **EXERCISE 39:** Use your own words to complete the dialogues with questions that begin with *why*, *when*, *what time*, and *where*.

1. A: ___*Where do you want to go for your vacation?*___
   B: Hawaii.

2. A: _____
   B: Ten o'clock.

3. A: _____
   B: Because I was tired.

4. A: _____
   B: Last week.

5. A: _____
   B: South America.

6. A: _____
   B: Because I forgot.

7. A: _____
   B: Downtown.

8. A: _____
   B: Several months ago.

9. A: _____
   B: At a Chinese restaurant.

5-14 QUESTIONS WITH *WHAT*

What is used in a question when you want to find out about a thing. *Who* is used when you want to find out about a person. (See Chart 5-15 for questions with *who*.)

(QUESTION + WORD)	HELPING + VERB	SUBJECT +	MAIN VERB		ANSWER
(a)	*Did*	Carol	*buy*	a car? →	*Yes, she did.* (She bought a car.)
(b) *What*	*did*	Carol	*buy*?	→	*A car.* (She bought a car.)
(c)	*Is*	Fred	*holding*	a book? →	*Yes, he is.* (He's holding a book.)
(d) *What*	*is*	Fred	*holding*?	→	*A book.* (He's holding a book.)

s v o (e) Carol bought *a car*.	In (e): *a car* is the object of the verb.
o v s v (f) *What* did Carol buy?	In (f): *what* is the object of the verb.

■ **EXERCISE 40:** Make questions.

1. A: ___*Did you buy a new tape recorder?*___
   B: Yes, I did. (I bought a new tape recorder.)

2. A: ___*What did you buy?*___
   B: A new tape recorder. (I bought a new tape recorder.)

3. A: _____
   B: Yes, she is. (Mary is carrying a suitcase.)

4. A: _____
   B: A suitcase. (Mary is carrying a suitcase.)

5. A: _____
   B: Yes, I do. (I see that airplane.)

6. A: _____
   B: An airplane. (I see an airplane.)

7. A: _____
   B: A hamburger. (Bob ate a hamburger for lunch.)

8. A: _____
   B: Yes, he did. (Bob ate a hamburger for lunch.)

9. A: _____
   B: A sandwich. (Bob usually eats a sandwich for lunch.)

10. A: _____
    B: No, he doesn't. (Bob doesn't like salads.)

■ **EXERCISE 41:** Make questions.

1. A: ___*What did John talk about?*___
   B: His country. (John talked about his country.)

2. A: ___*Did John talk about his country?*___
   B: Yes, he did. (John talked about his country.)

3. A: _____
   B: A bird. (I'm looking at a bird.)

4. A: _____
   B: Yes, I am. (I'm looking at that bird.)

5. A: _____
   B: Yes, I am. (I'm interested in science.)

6. A: _____
   B: Science. (I'm interested in science.)

7. A: _____
   B: Nothing in particular. (I'm thinking about nothing in particular.)

8. A: _____
   B: English grammar. (I dreamed about English grammar last night.)

9. A: _____
   B: The map on the wall. (The teacher is pointing at the map on the wall.)

10. A: _____
    B: No, I'm not. (I'm not afraid of snakes.) Are you?

■ **EXERCISE 42—ORAL (BOOKS CLOSED):** Ask a classmate a question. Use **what** and either a past or present verb.

Example: eat
STUDENT A: What did you eat for breakfast this morning? / What do you usually eat for dinner? / etc.
STUDENT A: *(free response)*

1. eat
2. wear
3. look at
4. study
5. think about
6. be interested in
7. be afraid of
8. dream about
9. have
10. need to buy

	QUESTION		ANSWER	
(a)	**What** did they see?	→	**A boat**. *(They saw a boat.)*	**What** is used to ask questions about things. **Who** is used to ask questions about people.
(b)	**Who** did they see?	→	**Jim**. *(They saw Jim.)*	

	QUESTION		ANSWER	
(c)	**Who** did they see?	→	**Jim**. *(They saw Jim.)*	(c) and (d) have the same meaning. **Whom** is used in formal English as the object of a verb or a preposition.
(d)	**Whom** did they see?	→	**Jim**. *(They saw Jim.)*	In (c): **who**, not **whom**, is usually used in everyday English. In (d): **whom** is used in very formal English. **Whom** is rarely used in everyday spoken English.

		O			O	
(e)	**Who(m)** did they see?	→		**Jim**. *(They saw **Jim**.)*		In (e): **who(m)** is the object of the verb. Usual question word order *(question word + helping verb + subject + main verb)* is used.

	S			S	
(f)	**Who** came?	→	**Mary**. (**Mary** came.)		In (f), (g), and (h): **who** is the subject of the question. Usual question word order is NOT used. When **who** is the subject of a question, do NOT use **does**, **do**, or **did**. Do NOT change the verb in any way: the verb form in the question is the same as the verb form in the answer. INCORRECT: *Who did come?*
(g)	**Who** lives there?	→	**Ed**. (**Ed** lives there.)		
(h)	**Who** saw Jim?	→	**Ann**. (**Ann** saw Jim.)		

■ **EXERCISE 43:** Make questions.

1. A: _____
   B: Mary. (I saw Mary at the party.)

2. A: _____
   B: Mary. (Mary came to the party.)

3. A: _____
   B: John. (John lives in that house.)

4. A: _____
   B: John. (I called John.)

5. A: _____
   B: My aunt and uncle. (I visited my aunt and uncle.)

6. A: _____
   B: My cousin. (My cousin visited me.)

7. A: _____
   B: Bob. (Bob helped Ann.)

8. A: _____
   B: Ann. (Bob helped Ann.)

9. A: _____
   B: Yes, he did. (Bob helped Ann.)

10. A: _____
    B: No, I'm not. (I'm not confused.)

■ **EXERCISE 44:** Make questions.

1. A: _____
   B: Ken. (I saw Ken.)

2. A: _____
   B: Ken. (I talked to Ken.)

3. A: _____
   B: Nancy. (I visited Nancy.)

4. A: _____
   B: Mary. (I'm thinking about Mary.)

5. A: _____
   B: Yuko. (Yuko called.)

6. A: _____
   B: Ahmed. (Ahmed answered the question.)

7. A: _____
   B: Mr. Lee. (Mr. Lee taught the English class.)

8. A: _____
   B: Carlos. (Carlos helped me.)

9. A: _____
   B. Gina. (I helped Gina.)

10. A: _____
    B: My brother. (My brother carried my suitcase.)

■ **EXERCISE 45:** Make questions. Use any appropriate question word: *where, when, what time, why, who, what*.

1. A: _____
   B: To the zoo. (Ann went to the zoo.)

2. A: _____
   B: Yesterday. (Ann went to the zoo yesterday.)

3. A: _____
   B: Ann. (Ann went to the zoo yesterday.)

4. A: _____
   B: Ali. (I saw Ali.)

5. A: _____
   B: At the zoo. (I saw Ali at the zoo.)

6. A: _____
   B: Yesterday. (I saw Ali at the zoo yesterday.)

7. A: _____
   B: Because the weather was nice. (I went to the zoo yesterday because the weather was nice.)

8. A: _____
   B: Dr. Jones. (I talked to Dr. Jones.)

9. A: _____
   B: Dr. Jones. (Dr. Jones called.)

10. A: _____
    B: Yesterday afternoon. (Dr. Jones called yesterday afternoon.)

11. A: _____
    B: At home. (I was at home yesterday afternoon.)

12. A: _____
    B: In an apartment. (I'm living in an apartment.)

13. A: _____
    B: Grammar. (The teacher is talking about grammar.)

14. A: _____
    B: A frog. (Annie has a frog in her pocket.)

(a) **What does** "pretty" **mean**?	(a) and (b) have the same meaning.
(b) **What is the meaning of** "pretty"?	INCORRECT: *What means "pretty"?*

■ **EXERCISE 46:** Ask a classmate for the meaning of the following words:

1. muggy	6. listen	11. discover	16. forest
2. awful	7. supermarket	12. simple	17. possess
3. quiet	8. crowd	13. empty	18. invite
4. century	9. lend	14. enjoy	19. modern
5. finish	10. murder	15. ill	20. pretty difficult

■ **EXERCISE 47:** Make questions. Use your own words.

1. A: _____
   B: Yesterday.

2. A: _____
   B: My brother.

3. A: _____
   B: A new pair of sandals.

4. A: _____
   B: At 7:30.

5. A: _____
   B: At Rossini's Restaurant.

6. A: _____
   B: This afternoon.

7. A: _____
   B: In an apartment.

8. A: _____
   B: My roommate.

9. A: _____
   B: Because I wanted to.

10. A: _____
    B: Ann.

11. A: _____
    B: A bird.

12. A: _____
    B: The zoo.

■ **EXERCISE 48—ORAL (BOOKS CLOSED):** Make questions that would produce the following answers.

Example: At 7 o'clock.
Response: When did you get up this morning? / What time does the movie start? / etc.

1. In an apartment.	11. Yes.
2. Yesterday.	12. Nothing.
3. It means "wonderful."	13. In the dormitory.
4. (. . .).	14. Because I was tired.
5. At seven-thirty.	15. (. . .).
6. A shirt.	16. At nine o'clock.
7. A hamburger.	17. A new pair of shoes.
8. No.	18. On *(name of a street in this city)*.
9. Because I wanted to.	19. In *(name of this state/province)*.
10. Grammar.	20. Last night.

5-17 MORE IRREGULAR VERBS

break - broke	*meet - met*	*sing - sang*
fly - flew	*pay - paid*	*speak - spoke*
hear - heard	*ring - rang*	*take - took*
leave - left	*send - sent*	*wake up - woke up*

■ **EXERCISE 49—ORAL (BOOKS CLOSED):** Practice using IRREGULAR VERBS.

Example: break-broke
TEACHER: break, broke. Sometimes a person breaks an arm or a leg. I broke my arm five years ago. What happened five years ago?
STUDENTS: break, broke. You broke your arm.
TEACHER: (to Student A) Did you ever break a bone?
STUDENT A: Yes. I broke my leg ten years ago.

1. *fly-flew*   Sometimes I fly home in an airplane. I flew home in an airplane last month. What did I do last month? When did you fly to this city?

2. *hear-heard*   I hear birds singing every morning. I heard birds singing yesterday. What did I do yesterday? What did you hear when you woke up this morning?

3. *pay-paid*   I pay the rent every month. I paid the rent last month. What did I do last month? Did you pay your rent last month?

4. *send-sent*   I send my mother a gift every year on her birthday. I sent my mother a gift last year on her birthday. What did I do last year? When did you send a gift to someone?

5. *leave-left*   I leave for school at 8:00 every morning. I left for school yesterday at 8:00 A.M. What did I do at 8:00 A.M. yesterday? What time did you leave for class this morning?

6. *meet-met*   I meet new people every week. Yesterday I met (. . .)'s friend. What did I do yesterday? Do you know (. . .)? When did you meet him/her?

7. *take-took*   I take my younger brother to the movies every month. I took my younger brother to the movies last month. What did I do last month? Who has a younger brother or sister? Where and when did you take him/her someplace?

8. *wake-woke*   I usually wake up at six. This morning I woke up at six-thirty. What time did I wake up this morning? What time did you wake up this morning?

9. *speak-spoke*   I speak to many students every day. Before class today, I spoke to (. . .). Who did I speak to? Who did you speak to before class today?

10. *ring-rang*   The phone in our apartment rings a lot. This morning it rang at six-thirty and woke me up. What happened at six-thirty this morning? Who had a telephone call this morning? What time did the phone ring?

11. *sing-sang*   I sing in the shower every morning. I sang in the shower yesterday. What did I do yesterday? Do you ever sing? When was the last time?

12. *break-broke*   Sometimes I break things. This morning I dropped a glass on the floor and it broke. What happened this morning? When did you break something?

■ **EXERCISE 50:**   Complete the sentences. Use the correct form of the words in the list.

break	*meet*	*sing*
fly	*pay*	*speak*
hear	*ring*	*take*
leave	*send*	*wake*

1. A: What happened to your finger?

   B: I _____ it in a soccer game.

2. A: Who did you talk to at the director's office?

   B: I _____ to the secretary.

3. A: When did Jessica leave for Europe?

   B: She _____ for Europe five days ago.

4. A: Did you write Ted a letter?

   B: No, but I _____ him a postcard.

5. A: Do you know Meg Adams?

   B: Yes. I _____ her a couple of weeks ago.

6. A: Why did you call the police?

   B: Because I _____ a burglar!

7. A: Where did you go yesterday?

   B: I _____ the children to the zoo.

8. A: What time did you get up this morning?
   B: 6:15.
   A: Why did you get up so early?

   B: The telephone _____.

9. A: Did you enjoy the party?

   B: Yes, I had a good time. We _____ songs and danced. It was fun.

10. A: You look sleepy.

    B: I am. I _____ up before dawn this morning and couldn't get back to sleep.

11. A: Did you give the painter a check?

    B: No. I _____ him in cash.

12. A: A bird _____ into our apartment yesterday through an open window.
    B: Really? What did you do?
    A: I caught it and took it outside.

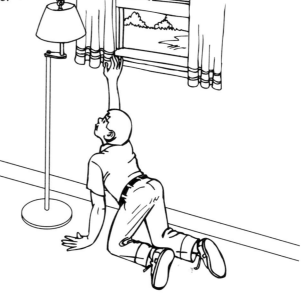

(a) $\overset{\text{S V}}{I\ ate\ breakfast.}$ = a main clause	A clause is a group of words that has a subject and a verb.
(b) ***before*** $\overset{\text{S V}}{I\ went\ to\ class}$ = a time clause	A main clause is a complete sentence. Example (a) is a complete sentence. Example (b) is an incomplete sentence. It must be connected to a main clause, as in (c) and (d).
(c) | I ate breakfast | $\overset{\text{S V}}{\|\ \textbf{\textit{before}}\ I\ went\ to\ class.\ \|}$ main clause time clause	

(d) $\|\ \overset{\text{S V}}{\textbf{\textit{Before}}\ I\ went\ to\ class,}\ \|$ | I ate breakfast. |
   time clause   main clause
	A time clause can begin with ***before*** or ***after***:
	    before + S + V = a time clause
	    after + S + V = a time clause

(e) | We took a walk | | ***after*** *we finished our work.* | main clause time clause	A time clause can follow a main clause, as in (c) and (e). A time clause can come in front of a main clause, as in (d) and (f). There is no difference in meaning between (c) and (d) or between (e) and (f).
(f) | ***After*** *we finished our work,* | | we took a walk. | time clause main clause	
(g) We took a walk | *after the movie.* | prep. phrase	***Before*** and ***after*** don't always introduce a time clause. They are also used as prepositions followed by a noun object, as in (g) and (h). See Charts 1-7 and 4-1 for information about prepositional phrases.
(h) I had a cup of coffee | *before class.* | prep. phrase	

■ **EXERCISE 51:** Find the main clauses and the time clauses.

    1. Before I ate the banana, I peeled it.
       →   *main clause = I peeled it*
       →   *time clause = before I ate the banana*

    2. We arrived at the airport before the plane landed.

    3. I went to a movie after I finished my homework.

    4. After the children got home from school, they watched TV.★

    5. Before I moved to this city, I lived at home with my parents.

★NOTE: When a time clause comes before the main clause, a comma is used between the two clauses. A comma is not used when the time clause comes after the main clause.

■ **EXERCISE 52:** Add a capital letter and period to the complete sentences. Write "*Inc.*" to mean "*Incomplete*" if the group of words is a time clause and not a complete sentence.

1. we went home → *W we went home.*

2. after we left my uncle's house → *Inc.*

3. we went home after we left my uncle's house
   → *W we went home after we left my uncle's house.*

4. before we ate our picnic lunch

5. we went to the zoo

6. we went to the zoo before we ate our picnic lunch

7. the children played games after they did their work

8. the children played games

9. after they did their work

10. the lions killed a zebra

11. after the lions killed a zebra

12. they ate it

13. after the lions killed a zebra, they ate it

■ **EXERCISE 53:** Combine the two ideas into one sentence by using *before* and *after* to introduce time clauses.

Example: I put on my coat. I went outside.
   → *Before I went outside, I put on my coat.*
   I put on my coat before I went outside.
   After I put on my coat, I went outside.
   I went outside after I put on my coat.

1. She ate breakfast.   She went to work.

2. He did his homework.   He went to bed.

3. We bought tickets.   We entered the theater.

■ **EXERCISE 54:** Use the given words to write sentences of your own. Use the SIMPLE PAST.

Example: after I
Written: I went to college after I graduated from high school.
After I finished dinner, I watched TV.
Etc.

1. before I came here
2. after I got home last night
3. I went . . . before I

4. after we
5. before they
6. Mr. . . . after he

5-19 *WHEN* IN TIME CLAUSES

(a) **When** *the rain stopped,* we took a walk. OR: We took a walk **when** *the rain stopped.*	**When** can introduce a time clause. **when** + S + V = a time clause In (a): **when** *the rain stopped* is a time clause.
(b) *When* **Tom** *was a child,* **he** *lived with his aunt.* OR: **Tom** *lived with his aunt* **when** *he was a child.*	In (b): Notice that the noun *(Tom)* comes before the pronoun *(he).*
COMPARE: (c) *When did the rain stop?* = a question (d) *when the rain stopped* = a time clause	**When** is also used to introduce questions.★ A question is a complete sentence, as in (c). A time clause is not a complete sentence.

★See Charts 2-12 and 5-13 for information about using *when* in questions.

■ **EXERCISE 55:** Choose the best completion. Then change the position of the time clause.

Example: When the phone rang,
→ When the phone rang, I answered it.★
I answered the phone when it rang.

1. When the phone rang,
2. When I was in Japan,
3. Maria bought some new shoes
4. I took a lot of photographs
5. When a stranger grabbed Ann's arm,
6. Jim was a wrestler
7. When the rain stopped,
8. The antique vase broke

A. she screamed.
B. when I dropped it.
C. I closed my umbrella.
D. when he was in high school.
✔ E. I answered it.
F. when she went shopping yesterday.
G. I stayed in a hotel in Tokyo.
H. when I was in Hawaii.

★NOTE: If a sentence with a *when*-clause talks about two actions, the action in the *when*-clause happens first. In the sentence *When the phone rang, I answered it:* first the phone rang, and then I answered it. Not logically possible: *When I answered the phone, it rang.*

■ **EXERCISE 56:** Add a capital letter and a question mark to complete the sentences. Write "*Inc.*" to mean "*Incomplete*" if the group of words is a time clause and not a question.

1. when did Jim arrive → ***W** when did Jim arrive?*

2. when Jim arrived → *Inc.*

3. when you were a child

4. when were you in Iran

5. when did the movie end

6. when the movie ended

7. when Mr. Wang arrived at the airport

8. when Khalid and Bakir went to a restaurant on First Street yesterday

9. when I was a high school student

10. when does the museum open

■ **EXERCISE 57:** Use the given words and your own words to create sentences. Don't change the order of the words.

1. When did . . . .   4. When were . . . .
2. When I . . . .   5. When the . . . .
3. I . . . when . . . .   6. The . . . when . . . .

■ **EXERCISE 58—REVIEW:** Complete the sentences. Use the words in parentheses.

(1)   Yesterday *(be)* _____ a terrible day. Everything *(go)*

(2)   _____ wrong. First, I *(oversleep)* _____.

(3)   My alarm clock *(ring, not)* _____. I *(wake)*

(4)   _____ up when I *(hear)*

(5)   _____ some noise outside my window.

(6)   It was 9:15. I *(get)* _____ dressed quickly.

(7)   I *(run)* _____ to class, but

(8)   I *(be)* _____ late. The teacher

(9)   *(be)* _____ upset. After my classes in the morning,

(10)   I *(go)* _____ to the cafeteria for lunch. I *(have)*

(11)   _____ an embarrassing accident at the cafeteria. I accidentally

(12)   *(drop)* _____ my tray of food. Some of the dishes *(break)*

(13)   _____. When I *(drop)* _____ the tray,

(14)   everyone in the cafeteria *(look)* _____ at me. I

(15)   *(go)* _____ back to the cafeteria line and

(16)   *(get)* _____ a second tray of food. I *(pay)*

(17)   _____ for my lunch again. After I *(sit)*

(18)   _____ down at a table in the corner by

(19)   myself, I *(eat)* _____ my sandwich and

(20)   *(drink)* _____ a cup of tea.

(21)   After lunch, I *(go)* _____ outside. I *(sit)* _____

(22)   under a tree near the classroom building. I *(see)* _____ a friend. I

(23)   *(call)* _____ to him. He

(24)   *(join)* _____ me on the grass.

(25)   We *(talk)* _____ about our

(26)   classes and *(relax)* _____.

       Everything was fine. But when I *(stand)*

(27)   _____ up, I *(step)*

(28)   _____ in a hole and *(break)*

(29)   _____ my ankle.

(30)   My friend *(drive)* _____ me to

(31)   the hospital. We *(go)* _____ to the

       emergency ward. After the doctor *(take)*

(32)   _____ X-rays of my ankle, he

(33)   *(put)* _____ a cast on it. I

(34) *(pay)* _____ my bill. Then we *(leave)* _____

(35) the hospital. My friend *(take)* _____ me home and *(help)*

(36) _____ me up the stairs to my apartment.

(37)   When we *(get)* _____ to the door of my apartment, I *(look)*

(38) _____ for my key. I *(look)* _____ in my

purse and in my pockets. There was no key. I *(ring)*

(39) _____ the doorbell. I *(think)*

(40) _____ that my roommate might be

(41) at home, but she *(be, not)* _____. So I *(sit)*

(42) _____ down on the floor outside my apartment

(43) and *(wait)* _____ for my roommate to get

home.

(44)   Finally, my roommate *(come)* _____ home and I *(get)*

(45) _____ into the apartment. I *(eat)* _____

(46) dinner quickly and *(go)* _____ to bed. I *(sleep)*

(47) _____ for ten hours. I hope today is a better day than yesterday!

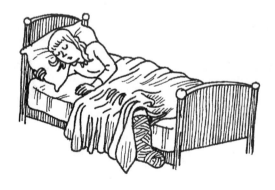

■ **EXERCISE 59—ORAL:** The person in the story in Exercise 58 is named Sara. Form small groups and tell the story of Sara's day. The first person in the group should say a few things about Sara's day. The next person should continue the story. And then the next. Pay special attention to the past form of the verbs.

    Glance at your book if you need to remember the story, but don't look at your book when you are speaking.

Example:

STUDENT A: Sara had a terrible day yesterday. Everything went wrong for her.
STUDENT B: Yes, she had a terrible day. First she overslept and miss class.
STUDENT C: Missed. She *missed* class.
STUDENT B: Right. She *missed* class.
STUDENT C: She missed class because her alarm clock didn't rang.
STUDENT D: Didn't *ring*, not rang.
STUDENT C: Right! Her alarm clock didn't *ring*.
STUDENT D: She woke up when she heard some noise outside her window at 9:15. She got dressed quickly and run to class.
STUDENT A: Excuse me, but I think you should say that she got dressed quickly and . . . .

■ **EXERCISE 60—WRITTEN:** Write the story of Sara's day. Don't look at your textbook. Write from memory.

■ **EXERCISE 61—WRITTEN:** Choose one of the topics and write a composition about past events. Use time expressions (*first, next, then, at . . . o'clock, later, after, before, when, etc.*) to show the order of the activities.

Topic 1: Write about your activities yesterday, from the time you got up to the time you went to bed.
Topic 2: Write about one of the best days in your life. What happened?
Topic 3: Write about one of the worst days in your life. What happened?

■ **EXERCISE 62—WRITTEN:** Interview someone you know about his/her activities yesterday morning, yesterday afternoon, and last night. Then use this information to write a composition. Use time expressions (*first, next, then, at . . . o'clock, later, after, before, when, etc.*) to show the order of the activities.

■ **EXERCISE 63—REVIEW:** Give the past form of the verbs.

1. visit	*visited*	10. pay	_____
2. fly	*flew*	11. catch	_____
3. go	_____	12. happen	_____
4. worry	_____	13. listen	_____
5. speak	_____	14. plan	_____
6. ride	_____	15. rain	_____
7. stand	_____	16. bring	_____
8. turn	_____	17. take	_____
9. hear	_____	18. write	_____

19. break	_____	25. ring	_____
20. stop	_____	26. meet	_____
21. hope	_____	27. leave	_____
22. sing	_____	28. occur	_____
23. think	_____	29. teach	_____
24. drive	_____	30. read	_____

■ **EXERCISE 64—REVIEW:**   Ask and answer questions using the SIMPLE PAST. Use the given verbs.

STUDENT A: Make up any question that includes the given verb. Use the SIMPLE PAST.
STUDENT B: Answer the question. Give a short answer and a long answer.

Example: speak
STUDENT A: Did you speak to Mr. Lee yesterday?
STUDENT B: Yes, I did. I spoke to him yesterday.

Example: finish
STUDENT A: What time did you finish your homework last night?
STUDENT B: Around nine o'clock. I finished my homework around nine o'clock.

Switch roles.

1. drink	5. fly	9. see	13. buy
2. eat	6. talk	10. sleep	14. send
3. study	7. wake up	11. work	15. watch
4. take	8. come	12. have	16. read

■ **EXERCISE 65— REVIEW:**   Correct the mistakes in the following.

1. Did you went downtown yesterday?

2. Yesterday I speak to Ken before he leaves his office and goes home.

3. I heared a good joke last night.

4. When Pablo finished his work.

5. I visitted my relatives in New York City last month.

6. Where you did go yesterday afternoon?

7. Ms. Wah was flew from Singapore to Tokyo last week.

8. When I see my friend yesterday, he didn't spoke to me.

9. Why Mustafa didn't came to class last week?

10. Where were you bought those shoes? I like them.

11. Mr. Adams teached our class last week.

12. I writed a letter last night.

13. Who you wrote a letter to?

14. Who did open the door? Jack openned it.

■ **EXERCISE 66—REVIEW:** Complete the sentences with the words in parentheses. Use the SIMPLE PRESENT, PRESENT PROGRESSIVE, or SIMPLE PAST. The sentence may require STATEMENT, NEGATIVE, or QUESTION FORMS.

1. Tom *(walk)* _____ *walks* _____ to work almost every day.

2. I can see Tom from my window. He's on the street below. He *(walk)*

   _____ to work right now.

3. *(Tom, walk)* _____ to work every day?

4. *(you, walk)* _____ to work every day?

5. I usually take the bus to work, but yesterday I *(walk)* _____ to my office.

6. On my way to work yesterday, I *(see)* _____ an accident.

7. Alex *(see, not)* _____ the accident.

8. *(you, see)* _____ the accident yesterday?

9. Tom *(walk, not)* _____ to work when the weather is cold. He *(take)*

   _____ the bus.

10. I *(walk, not)* _____ to work in cold weather either.

■ **EXERCISE 67—REVIEW:** Complete the sentences with the words in parentheses.

(1)   Yesterday Fish *(be)* _____ in the river. He *(see)* _____

Bear on the bank of the river. Here is their conversation.

BEAR: Good morning, Fish.

(2) FISH: Good morning, Bear. How *(you, be)* _____ today?

(3) BEAR: I *(do)* _____ fine, thank you. And you?

FISH: Fine, thanks.

(4) BEAR: *(you, would like)* _____ to get out of the river and *(sit)*

(5) _____ with me? I *(need)* _____ someone to talk to.

(6) FISH: I *(need, not)* _____ to get out of the river for us to talk.

We can talk just the way we are now.

BEAR: Hmmm.

(7) FISH: Wait! What *(you, do)* _____?

(8) BEAR: I *(get)* _____ in the river to join you.

(9) FISH: Stop! This *(be)* _____ my river! I *(trust, not)* _____

(10) _____ you. What *(you, want)* _____?

(11) BEAR: Nothing. Just a little conversation. I *(want)* _____ to tell you about

(12) my problems. I *(have)* _____ a bad day yesterday.

FISH: Oh? What happened?

(13)   BEAR: While I was walking through the woods, I *(see)* _____ a beehive. I

(14)   *(love)* _____ honey. So I *(stop)* _____ at the

beehive. When I *(reach)*

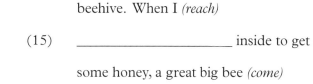

(15)   _____ inside to get

some honey, a great big bee *(come)*

(16)   _____ up behind

me and stung⋆ my ear. The sting

(17)   *(be)* _____ very painful.

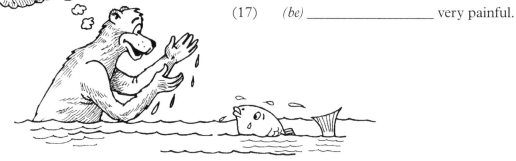

(18)   FISH: I *(believe, not)* _____ you. Bees can't hurt bears. I

(19)   *(believe, not)* _____ your story about a great big bee.

(20)   All bees *(be)* _____ the same size, and they *(be, not)* _____ big.

(21)   BEAR: But it *(be)* _____ true! Here. Come a little closer and look at

my ear. I'll show you where the big bee stung it.

(22)   FISH: Okay. Where *(it, be)* _____? Where *(the bee, sting)*

(23)   _____ you?

BEAR: Right here. See?

(24)   FISH: Stop! What *(you, do)* _____? Let go of me! Why

(25)   *(you, hold)* _____ me?

⋆*Stung* is the past form of the verb *sting,* which means "to cause sharp pain."

(26) BEAR: I *(hold)* _____ you because I'm going to eat you for dinner.

(27) FISH: Oh no! You *(trick)* _____ me! Your story about the great big bee

(28) never *(happen)* _____!

(29) BEAR: That's right. I *(get)* _____ in the river because I *(want)*

(30) _____ *(catch)* _____ you for dinner. And I

(31) did. I *(catch)* _____ you for dinner.

FISH: Watch out! Behind you! Oh no! Oh no! It's a very, very big bee. It's huge! It

(32) *(look)* _____ really angry!

(33) BEAR: I *(believe, not)* _____ you!

(34) FISH: But it *(be)* _____ true! A great big bee *(come)* _____

toward you. It's going to attack you and sting you!

(35) BEAR: What? Where? I *(see, not)* _____ a big bee! Oh no, Fish, you

(36) are getting away from me. Oh no! I *(drop)* _____ you! Come

back! Come back!

(37) FISH: Ha! I *(fool)* _____ you too, Bear. Now you must find your

dinner in another place.

(38) BEAR: Yes, you *(trick)* _____ me too. We *(teach)* _____

each other a good lesson today: Don't believe everything you hear.

FISH: Thank you for teaching me that lesson. Now I will live a long and happy life.

(39) BEAR: Yes, we *(learn)* _____ a good lesson today, and that's good. But

(40) I *(be)* _____ still hungry. Hmmm. I *(have)* _____

(41) a gold tooth in my mouth. *(you, would like)* _____ to

come closer and look at it?

The English Alphabet

A	a		N	n
B	b		O	o
C	c		P	p
D	d		Q	q
E	e		R	r
F	f		S	s
G	g		T	t
H	h		U	u
I	i		V	v
J	j		W	w
K	k		X	x
L	l		Y	y
M	m		Z	z★

Vowels = *a, e, i, o u.*
Consonants = *b, c, d, f, g, h, j, k, l, m, n, p, q, r, s, t, v, w, x, y, z.*

★The letter "z" is pronounced "zee" in American English and "zed" in British English.

APPENDIX 2
Numbers

1	one	1st	first
2	two	2nd	second
3	three	3rd	third
4	four	4th	fourth
5	five	5th	fifth
6	six	6th	sixth
7	seven	7th	seventh
8	eight	8th	eighth
9	nine	9th	ninth
10	ten	10th	tenth
11	eleven	11th	eleventh
12	twelve	12th	twelfth
13	thirteen	13th	thirteenth
14	fourteen	14th	fourteenth
15	fifteen	15th	fifteenth
16	sixteen	16th	sixteenth
17	seventeen	17th	seventeenth
18	eighteen	18th	eighteenth
19	nineteen	19th	nineteenth
20	twenty	20th	twentieth
21	twenty-one	21st	twenty-first
22	twenty-two	22nd	twenty-second
23	twenty-three	23rd	twenty-third
24	twenty-four	24th	twenty-fourth
25	twenty-five	25th	twenty-fifth
26	twenty-six	26th	twenty-sixth
27	twenty-seven	27th	twenty-seventh
28	twenty-eight	28th	twenty-eighth
29	twenty-nine	29th	twenty-ninth
30	thirty	30th	thirtieth
40	forty	40th	fortieth
50	fifty	50th	fiftieth
60	sixty	60th	sixtieth
70	seventy	70th	seventieth
80	eighty	80th	eightieth
90	ninety	90th	ninetieth
100	one hundred	100th	one hundredth
200	two hundred	200th	two hundredth
1,000	one thousand		
10,000	ten thousand		
100,000	one hundred thousand		
1,000,000	one million		

APPENDIX 3

Days of the Week and Months of the Year

DAYS

Monday	(Mon.)
Tuesday	(Tues.)
Wednesday	(Wed.)
Thursday	(Thurs.)
Friday	(Fri.)
Saturday	(Sat.)
Sunday	(Sun.)

MONTHS

January	(Jan.)
February	(Feb.)
March	(Mar.)
April	(Apr.)
May	(May)
June	(June)
July	(July)
August	(Aug.)
September	(Sept.)
October	(Oct.)
November	(Nov.)
December	(Dec.)

Using numbers to write the date:

month/day/year
10/31/41 = October 31, 1941
4/15/92 = April 15, 1992

Saying dates:

USUAL WRITTEN FORM	USUAL SPOKEN FORM
January 1	January first/the first of January
March 2	March second/the second of March
May 3	May third/the third of May
June 4	June fourth/the fourth of June
August 5	August fifth/the fifth of August
October 10	October tenth/the tenth of October
November 27	November twenty-seventh/the twenty-seventh of November

Ways of Saying the Time

9:00	It's nine o'clock.
	It's nine.
9:05	It's nine-oh-five.
	It's five (minutes) after nine.
	It's five (minutes) past nine.
9:10	It's nine-ten.
	It's ten (minutes) after nine.
	It's ten (minutes) past nine.
9:15	It's nine-fifteen.
	It's a quarter after nine.
	It's a quarter past nine.
9:30	It's nine-thirty.
	It's half past nine.
9:45	It's nine-forty-five.
	It's a quarter to ten.
	It's a quarter of ten.
9:50	It's nine-fifty.
	It's ten (minutes) to ten.
	It's ten (minutes) of ten.
12:00	It's noon.
	It's midnight.

A.M. = morning   It's nine A.M.
P.M. = afternoon/evening/night   It's nine P.M.

APPENDIX 5

Irregular Verbs

SIMPLE FORM	SIMPLE PAST	PAST PARTICIPLE	SIMPLE FORM	SIMPLE PAST	PAST PARTICIPLE
be	was, were	been	keep	kept	kept
become	became	become	know	knew	known
begin	began	begun	lend	lent	lent
bend	bent	bent	leave	left	left
bite	bit	bitten	lose	lost	lost
blow	blew	blown	make	made	made
break	broke	broken	meet	met	met
bring	brought	brought	pay	paid	paid
build	built	built	put	put	put
buy	bought	bought	read	read	read
catch	caught	caught	ride	rode	ridden
choose	chose	chosen	ring	rang	rung
come	came	come	run	ran	run
cost	cost	cost	say	said	said
cut	cut	cut	see	saw	seen
do	did	done	sell	sold	sold
draw	drew	drawn	send	sent	sent
drink	drank	drunk	shake	shook	shaken
drive	drove	driven	shut	shut	shut
eat	ate	eaten	sing	sang	sung
fall	fell	fallen	sit	sat	sat
feed	fed	fed	sleep	slept	slept
feel	felt	felt	speak	spoke	spoken
fight	fought	fought	spend	spent	spent
find	found	found	stand	stood	stood
fly	flew	flown	steal	stole	stolen
forget	forgot	forgotten	swim	swam	swum
get	got	gotten/got	take	took	taken
give	gave	given	teach	taught	taught
go	went	gone	tear	tore	torn
grow	grew	grown	tell	told	told
hang	hung	hung	think	thought	thought
have	had	had	throw	threw	thrown
hear	heard	heard	understand	understood	understood
hide	hid	hidden	wake up	woke up	woken up
hit	hit	hit	wear	wore	worn
hold	held	held	win	won	won
hurt	hurt	hurt	write	wrote	written

Index